SKILL SHARPENERS
Math 4

Keep Your Child's Academic Skills Sharp

This book belongs to

_____

name

Writing: Vicky Shiotsu
Content Editing: Kathleen Jorgensen
Copy Editing: Cathy Harber
Art Direction: Yuki Meyer
Illustration: Bryan Langdo
Design/Production: Jessica Onken

EMC 8254

Evan-Moor®

Visit
teaching-standards.com
to view a correlation
of this book.
This is a free service.

**Correlated to
Current Standards**

**Congratulations on your purchase of some of the
finest teaching materials in the world.**

Evan-Moor Corporation
phone 1-800-777-4362, fax 1-800-777-4332.
Entire contents © 2020 Evan-Moor Corporation
18 Lower Ragsdale Drive, Monterey, CA 93940-5746. Printed in China.

CPSIA: Asia Pacific Offset Ltd, Kowloon, Hong Kong [1/2022]

Dear student,

Math is all around us. If you want to know "**how long**," "**how fast**," "**what part**," or "**what size**," you need math! This fun workbook will help you practice.

Many pages show you objects to help you add, subtract, multiply, divide, and make fractions. You can use real objects, too!

There are lots of ways to solve problems. Some are shown in an example on the page. Study the example and try it, or use your favorite strategy.

Some of the problems are word problems that tell a short story. Put yourself in the story to solve them.

If you <u>get stuck</u>, ask yourself these questions:

★ What is the goal of the problem?

★ What information do I have already?

★ What do these numbers have to do with each other?

★ Should I add, subtract, multiply, or divide?

★ Do I need to figure out another number before I can find the answer?

When you finish this workbook, your skills will be **super sharp!**

Sincerely,

Your friends at Evan-Moor

Contents

A Fun Field Trip

Read about a fun field trip and solve the problems.

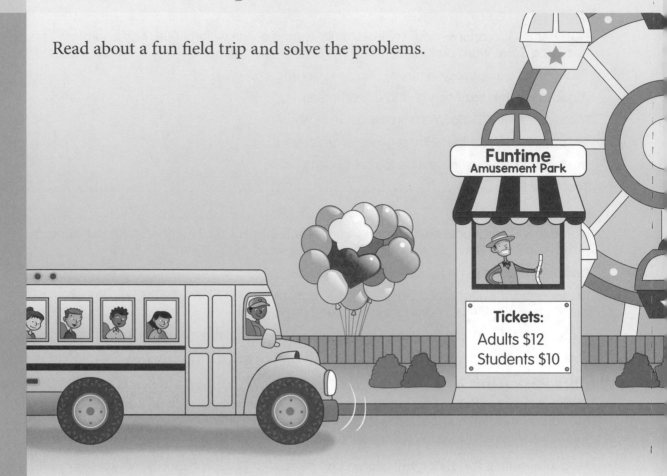

Funtime
Amusement Park

Tickets:
Adults $12
Students $10

Amusement Park

1. It is $25\frac{1}{2}$ miles from the school to the amusement park. How many miles will the round trip be?   _____ miles

2. There are 98 students and 12 adults. They will ride on two buses. Each bus will hold the same number of riders. How many riders will be on each bus?   _____ riders

3. How much will the tickets cost? $_____

4. The bus drivers charge $20 for the first hour and $16 for each additional hour. The buses will leave the school at 9:00 a.m. and return at 3:00 p.m. How much will each of the two bus drivers be paid? $_____

5. What is the total cost of the field trip? $_____

Draw a path to help the children reach the rides. Begin at **Start**. Stop at each circled number. Decide whether it is odd or even and take the path that matches. Continue until you reach the park.

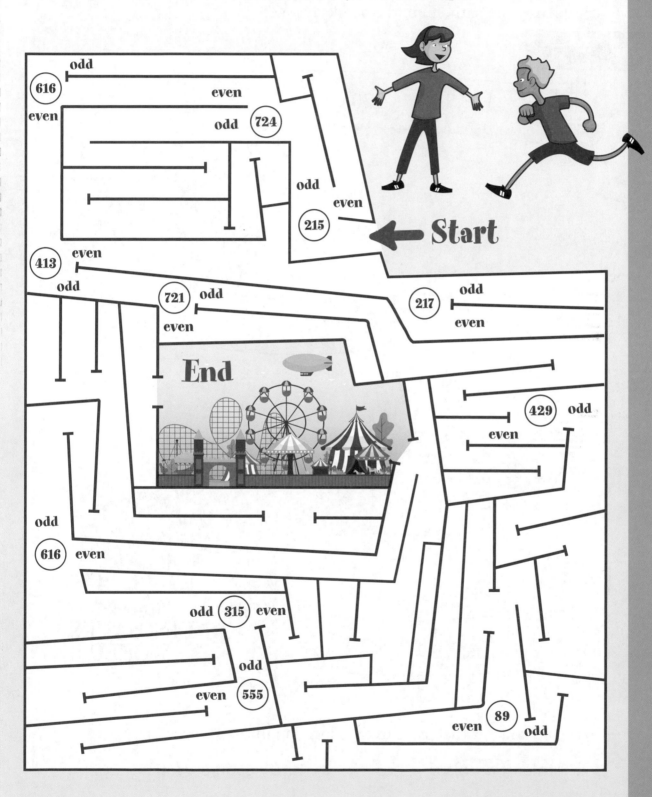

Amusement Park

Wonderlands

Start at the park's entrance. The first problem reads **8 × 3**. The answer goes in the next space. Then subtract **20**. Write that answer in the next empty space, and continue this pattern around the path. After completing the path, fill in the blanks below.

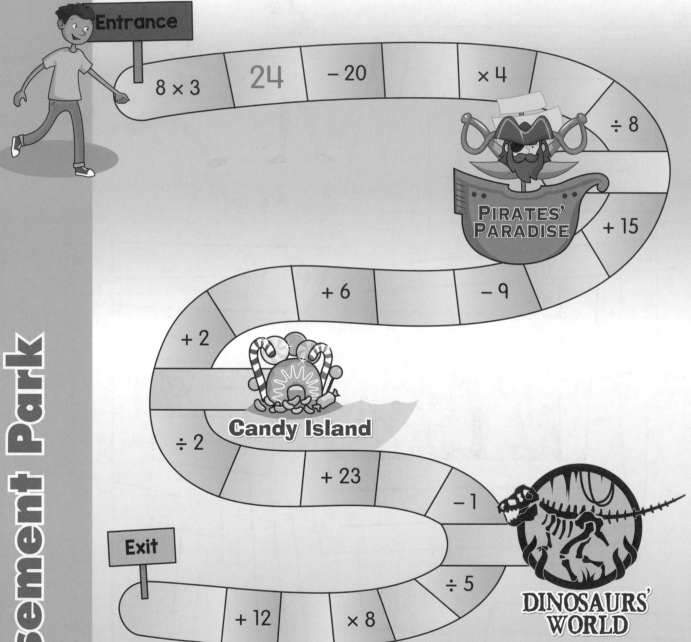

Amusement Park

Write the answer that leads to each location in the amusement park.

1. Pirates' Paradise: _____   3. Dinosaurs' World: _____

2. Candy Island: _____   4. Exit: _____

Mystery Ride

Find out which ride Reynaldo went on first. Solve the problems. Then write the matching letters in order on the lines at the bottom of the page.

1. 6 × 40 = _____

2. 3 × 50 = _____

3. 5 × 90 = _____

4. 60 × 7 = _____

5. 70 × 8 = _____

6. 90 × 6 = _____

7. 2 × 200 = _____

8. 3 × 300 = _____

9. 200 × 4 = _____

10. 200 × 3 = _____

150 = **U**	540 = **E**
240 = **J**	560 = **L**
300 = **F**	600 = **E**
400 = **R**	640 = **M**
420 = **G**	750 = **C**
450 = **N**	800 = **D**
500 = **T**	900 = **I**

____ ____ ____ ____ ____

____ ____ ____ ____

Amusement Park

Number Challenge

Skill:
Compose and decompose numbers

Use the numbers in each set to make the largest number possible. Then write each digit on the correct line to show its value.

1. 7, 6, 9, 2, 4

   number: _____

   _____ ten thousands

   _____ thousands

   _____ hundreds

   _____ tens

   _____ ones

2. 9, 4, 0, 7, 0

   number: _____

   _____ ten thousands

   _____ thousands

   _____ hundreds

   _____ tens

   _____ ones

3. 3, 5, 3, 0, 8

   number: _____

   _____ ten thousands

   _____ thousands

   _____ hundreds

   _____ tens

   _____ ones

4. 4, 0, 6, 2, 5

   number: _____

   _____ ten thousands

   _____ thousands

   _____ hundreds

   _____ tens

   _____ ones

5. 2, 9, 3, 9, 4

   number: _____

   _____ ten thousands

   _____ thousands

   _____ hundreds

   _____ tens

   _____ ones

Skill Sharpeners: Math • EMC 8254 • © Evan-Moor Corp.

Amusement Park

Skill:
Write numbers in standard and expanded form

Write each number in standard form.

1. ten thousand five   10,005

2. ten thousand fifty   _____

3. one hundred thousand five   _____

4. thirty-one thousand ten   _____

5. three hundred one thousand one hundred   _____

Write each number in standard form.

6. 2,000 + 100 + 60 + 3   2,163

7. 40,000 + 600 + 30   _____

8. 90,000 + 7,000 + 100 + 50 + 6   _____

9. 200,000 + 80,000 + 5,000 + 50   _____

10. 700,000 + 60,000 + 300 + 10 + 9   _____

Write each number in expanded form.

11. 27,108 _____ 20,000 + 7,000 + 100 + 8 _____

12. 19,375 _____

13. 836,954 _____

14. 603,737 _____

TICKETS

Amusement Park

11

Colorful Balloons

Write **>** or **<** between the balloons to compare the two numbers.

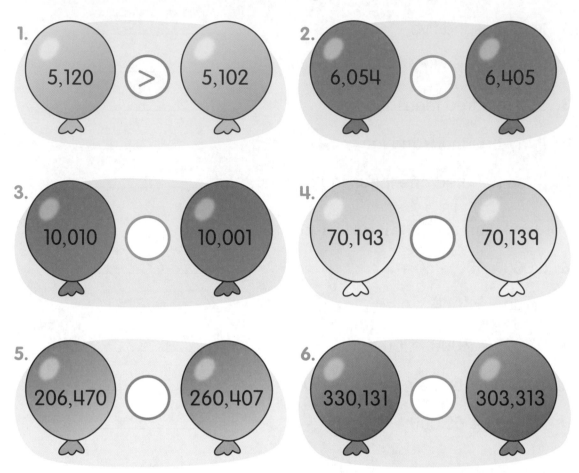

1. 5,120 **>** 5,102

2. 6,054 ○ 6,405

3. 10,010 ○ 10,001

4. 70,193 ○ 70,139

5. 206,470 ○ 260,407

6. 330,131 ○ 303,313

7. Read the clues. Write the child's name under the correct balloon.

- The **7** in Nik's number is 100 times greater than the **7** in Claudia's number.

- The **7** in Nik's number is 10 times greater than the **7** in Yuki's number.

- The **7** in Luca's number has the least value of any of the **7**s.

 207,105

 25,107

 701,520

 72,051

_____ _____ _____ _____

Skill Sharpeners: Math • EMC 8254 • © Evan-Moor Corp.

Amusement Park

Skill:
Identify fractions

The pizza parlor at the amusement park serves lunch every day. Look at each pizza plate and write the fraction that represents the leftover pizza.

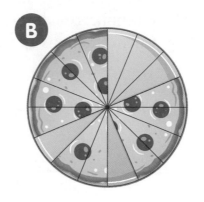

A

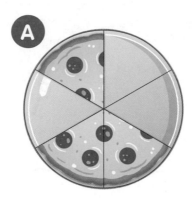

B

_____   _____

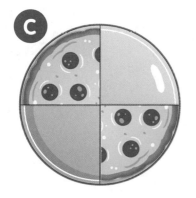

C

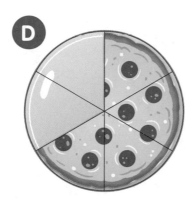

D

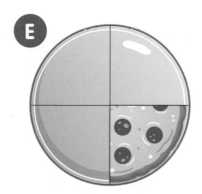

E

_____   _____   _____

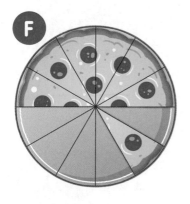

F

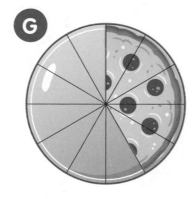

G

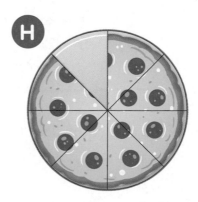

H

_____   _____   _____

Look at the pizzas.
Which two show equivalent amounts? _____

Amusement Park

A Magic Show

Use multiplication to make equivalent fractions appear!

$$\frac{1}{2} = \frac{1 \times 3}{2 \times 3} = \frac{3}{6}$$

1. $\frac{1}{4} = \frac{1 \times 2}{4 \times 2} = $

5. $\frac{3}{4} = \frac{3 \times 3}{4 \times 3} = $

2. $\frac{1}{3} = \frac{1 \times 3}{3 \times 3} = $

6. $\frac{2}{3} = \frac{2 \times 2}{3 \times 2} = $

3. $\frac{1}{2} = \frac{1 \times 4}{2 \times 4} = $

7. $\frac{3}{5} = \frac{3 \times 3}{5 \times 3} = $

4. $\frac{1}{5} = \frac{1 \times 2}{5 \times 2} = $

8. $\frac{1}{6} = \frac{1 \times 2}{6 \times 2} = $

Write two equivalent fractions for each fraction.

9. $\frac{1}{8}$

10. $\frac{4}{5}$

Circle the fraction in each set that is **not** equivalent to the others.

11. $\frac{1}{4}$ $\frac{3}{12}$ $\frac{2}{16}$ $\frac{5}{20}$

12. $\frac{1}{3}$ $\frac{2}{6}$ $\frac{4}{12}$ $\frac{6}{15}$

Skill Sharpeners: Math • EMC 8254 • © Evan-Moor Corp.

Skill:
Determine area

Two singers perform at the amusement park. They sing in the center of a stage. Colorful tiles make up the rest of the stage. Each whole tile is a square with sides that measure 1 foot.

1. What is the area covered by the blue tiles? _____ square feet

2. What is the area covered by the green tiles? _____ square feet

3. What is the total area of the tiles? _____ square feet

4. What is the area of the total stage, including the white part in the center? _____ square feet

   How do you know? _____

   _____

   _____

Amusement Park

A Great Time

Solve the problems.

1. Jesse looked at his watch and said, "I have 1 hour and 36 minutes left to go on rides before I need to leave." Jesse needs to leave at 2:00 p.m. At what time did he look at his watch?

   _____

2. Rachel rode the roller coaster 3 times! Each time she waited in line for 7 minutes and went on the ride for 3 minutes. Rachel got in line for the first ride at 10:45 a.m. At what time did she get off the ride the third time?

   _____

3. The magic show was going to start at 2:15 p.m. Arjay said, "I have lots of time. It's only 11:35 a.m." How much time did he have before the show started?

   _____ hours and _____ minutes

4. Tasneem spent 15 minutes playing Ring Toss, 12 minutes playing Roll 'n' Bowl, and 9 minutes playing Pop the Balloon. She finished playing at 11:05 a.m. At what time did Tasneem start the first game?

   _____

5. Keisha went on 8 rides, one after the other. Each ride, including the wait time, took 17 minutes. How long did she spend on rides?

   _____ hours and _____ minutes

6. Rodrigo and Bob spent 46 minutes exploring Dino World. Then they spent 25 minutes at Treasure Paradise before meeting the rest of their class at 1:30 p.m. At what time did they arrive at Dino World?

   _____

Amusement Park

Multiply.

60	50	40	200	300	400
× 3	× 8	× 6	× 3	× 3	× 2

Write each number in standard form.

thirty-six thousand five hundred one _____

nine thousand eight hundred sixteen _____

four hundred six thousand sixty-four _____

Circle the odd numbers.

106   125

247   591

Write each number in expanded form.

57,190 _____

806,073 _____

110,011 _____

Write a fraction to describe the part that is blue.

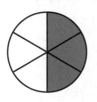

_____   _____   _____

Solve the problem.

Lee spent 4 hours and 23 minutes at the amusement park. She arrived at 9:55 a.m. At what time did she leave?

_____

Circle the fraction in each set that is **not** equivalent to the others.

$\dfrac{1}{4}$ $\dfrac{2}{8}$ $\dfrac{3}{10}$ $\dfrac{4}{16}$ | $\dfrac{2}{3}$ $\dfrac{5}{6}$ $\dfrac{6}{9}$ $\dfrac{8}{12}$

Skills:
Solve word problems; Add and subtract within 10,000

Solve the problems.

Newton School is holding a Math-a-thon. The goal is for students to complete a total of 6,000 math problems. They have done 3,090 problems so far. How many more problems do they need to complete?

_____ problems

Some students collected bottles for recycling. The first month, they collected 1,580 bottles. The next month, they collected 2,540 bottles. How many bottles did they collect in the first two months?

_____ bottles

Last week, 1,100 people went to Newton School's Open House. There were 485 students. The rest were parents. How many parents attended the Open House?

_____ parents

The fourth-grade students sold 275 magazines for a fundraiser. The fifth-grade students sold 195 more. How many magazines did the fourth- and fifth-grade students sell?

_____ magazines

Jamal read 139 more minutes in March than in February. He read 1,005 minutes in March. How many minutes did he read in February?

_____ minutes

Last month, students who read 1,000 minutes in 4 weeks won a book. Tasha read 235 minutes the first week. Each week she read 10 more minutes than the week before. Did she win a book?

_____

Four friends are playing a new computer game at school. The winner is the first player to reach 10,000 points. Look at the computer screen to see how many points they have so far. Then answer the questions.

Sabrina	9,876
Raul	9,590
Callie	9,651
Keanu	9,963

Skill:
Add and subtract within 10,000

Who has the highest score? _____

Who has the lowest score? _____

What is the difference in their scores? _____

How many points do Sabrina and Callie have in all?

_____

How many points do Raul and Keanu have in all?

_____

How many more points does the leader need to win?

_____ points

Write another problem using the information on the computer screen. Then solve your problem.

School Days

Skill:

Multiply
a multidigit
number by
a 1-digit
number

Help Kareem with his homework.

18 × 4	12 × 5	15 × 6	12 × 7
26 × 9	59 × 7	83 × 6	74 × 8
321 × 4	106 × 6	452 × 2	216 × 6
425 × 7	316 × 6	527 × 4	411 × 9
2,013 × 6	4,252 × 2	3,042 × 6	1,124 × 4

Solve the problems.

Show Your Work

1. There are 7 classrooms. Each one has 120 textbooks. How many textbooks are there in all?

   _____ textbooks

   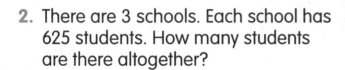

2. There are 3 schools. Each school has 625 students. How many students are there altogether?

   _____ students

3. One principal holds 8 assemblies a year. Each one lasts 115 minutes. How many minutes is that in all?

   _____ minutes

4. A school year is made up of 180 days. Sarah went to school 6 years without missing a day. How many days was that altogether?

   _____ days

5. There are 1,247 students. Each one has 4 notebooks. How many notebooks do they have in all?

   _____ notebooks

6. Six schools each spent $3,500 for new playground equipment. How much money was spent in all?

   $_____

School Days

Skill:
Divide within 100

Write the answers on the path to help Terry get to school.

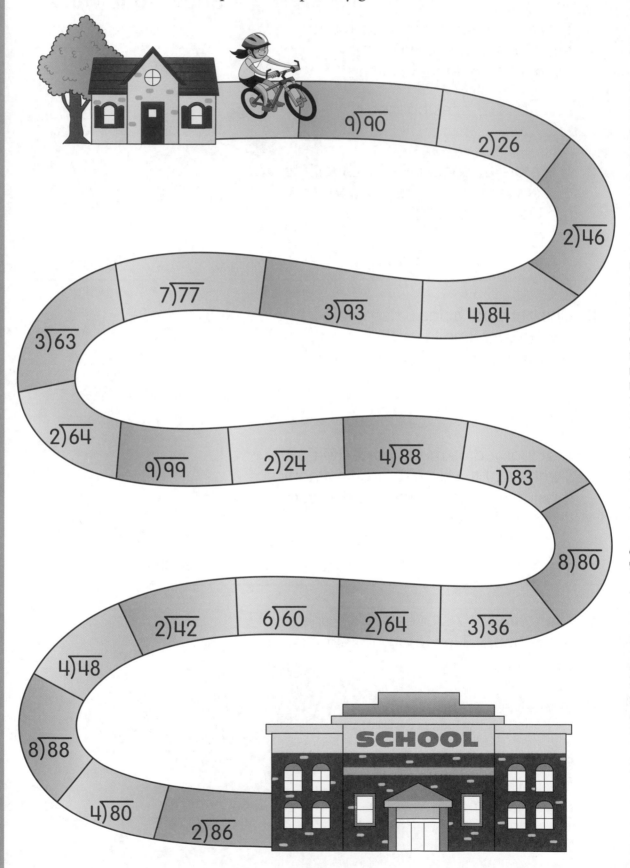

Skill Sharpeners: Math • EMC 8254 • © Evan-Moor Corp.

School Days

Divide. Then use multiplication to check your division.

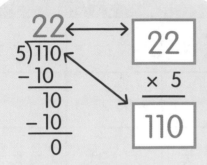

$$\begin{array}{r} 22 \\ 5\overline{)110} \\ -10 \\ \hline 10 \\ -10 \\ \hline 0 \end{array}$$

22
× 5
110

$7\overline{)217}$

☐
× 7
☐

$2\overline{)468}$

☐
× 2
☐

$6\overline{)726}$

☐
× 6
☐

$4\overline{)880}$

☐
× 4
☐

$9\overline{)459}$

☐
× 9
☐

$3\overline{)639}$

☐
× 3
☐

$8\overline{)344}$

☐
× 8
☐

Skills:

Divide within 1,000; Recognize the relationship between multiplication and division

School Days

Skill:
Interpret a picture graph

Use the graph to answer the questions.

Number of Children Playing Games at Recess

Game	Monday	Tuesday	Wednesday	Thursday	Friday
four square	👤👤👤👤	👤👤👤	👤👤👤	👤👤	👤👤👤
tag	👤		👤	👤👤	
dodge ball	👤👤👤	👤👤👤👤	👤👤👤	👤👤👤	👤👤👤👤👤
basketball	👤👤	👤👤	👤👤👤	👤👤	👤👤👤

👤 = 5 children

1. Which game was the most popular? _____

2. Which game was the least popular? _____

3. How many children played basketball during the week? _____ children

4. How many children played games at recess on Monday? _____ children

5. How many more children played dodge ball than four square on Friday?

   _____ more

6. On which day did the greatest number of children play games at recess?

   _____

   How many children played that day?

   _____ children

School Days

Some students drew shapes in art class. The shapes below have **symmetry**. A line can be drawn on each figure so that the two halves match exactly. On some figures, more than one line can be drawn.

Draw lines of symmetry on each figure. Then write how many lines of symmetry the figure has.

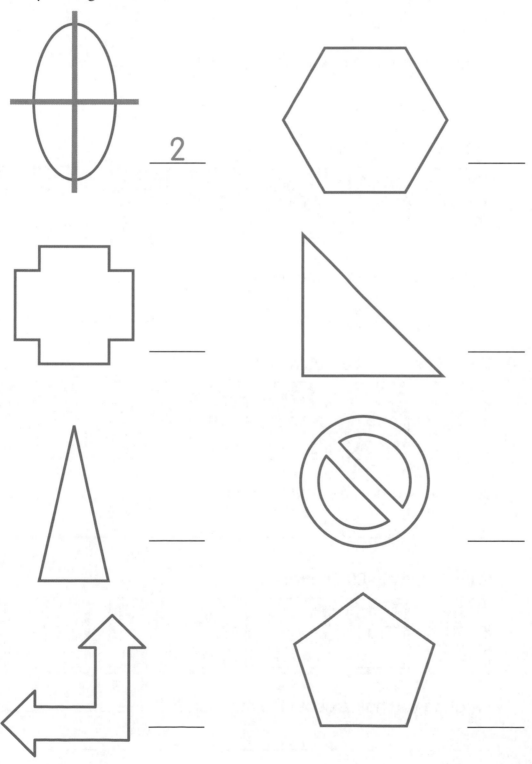

Skill:
Draw lines
of symmetry

School Days

Read the rule. Then extend the pattern by writing three more numbers.

1. **Rule:** Start with 4. Add 5.

What do you notice about the numbers? _____

_____

2. **Rule:** Start with 3. Add 10.

What do you notice about the numbers? _____

_____

3. **Rule:** Start with 100. Subtract 2.

What do you notice about the numbers? _____

_____

4. **Rule:** Start with 90. Subtract 9.

What do you notice about the numbers? _____

_____

Fractions and Number Lines

You can use a number line to compare fractions.

Example: Compare $\frac{3}{10}$ and $\frac{3}{4}$.

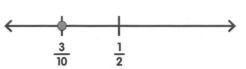

Plot each fraction on the number line.
Use the fraction $\frac{1}{2}$ to help you.
$\frac{3}{10}$ is less than $\frac{1}{2}$ and $\frac{3}{4}$ is greater than $\frac{1}{2}$.

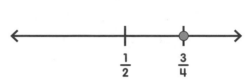

$\frac{3}{10}$ $\enclose{circle}{<}$ $\frac{3}{4}$

Plot the fractions on the number line.
Write **>**, **<**, or **=** to compare the fractions.

1. $\frac{3}{5}$ ← | → $\frac{1}{2}$

   $\frac{3}{8}$ ← | → $\frac{1}{2}$

   $\frac{3}{5}$ ◯ $\frac{3}{8}$

2. $\frac{1}{4}$ ← | → $\frac{1}{2}$

   $\frac{2}{3}$ ← | → $\frac{1}{2}$

   $\frac{1}{4}$ ◯ $\frac{2}{3}$

3. $\frac{5}{10}$ ← | → $\frac{1}{2}$

   $\frac{5}{6}$ ← | → $\frac{1}{2}$

   $\frac{5}{10}$ ◯ $\frac{5}{6}$

4. $\frac{3}{4}$ ← | → $\frac{1}{2}$

   $\frac{6}{8}$ ← | → $\frac{1}{2}$

   $\frac{3}{4}$ ◯ $\frac{6}{8}$

5. Kai lives $\frac{4}{5}$ mile from school. Joy lives $\frac{4}{8}$ mile from school.
   Who lives farther from school? How do you know?

_____

School Days

Skills:
Convert measurements (metric units); Determine area and perimeter

Use the information in the box to help you solve the problems.

Metric Units of Length
10 millimeters (mm) = 1 centimeter (cm)
100 centimeters = 1 meter (m)
1,000 meters = 1 kilometer (km)

1. Mrs. Kami's students measured their shadows at 9:00 a.m. and at noon. Megan's shadow was 85 cm longer at 9:00 than at noon.

   Megan's shadow was 135 centimeters at noon. How long was it at 9:00? _____

   Was her 9:00 shadow longer than or shorter than 2 meters? _____

2. Mr. Franklin's students tested how far their paper airplanes flew. Vanessa's plane flew 620 centimeters. Shawn's plane flew $6\frac{1}{2}$ meters.

   Whose plane flew farther? _____

   How much farther did that plane fly? _____

3. Yoshi learned that a threadsnake is 10 centimeters long.

   How many millimeters is that? _____

   Is it longer or shorter than a garter snake that is a half meter long? _____

4. Jayden made a poster to advertise the science fair. The poster was 2 meters tall and 1 meter wide. What was its perimeter in meters, centimeters, and millimeters?

   _____ m   _____ cm   _____ mm

Skill Sharpeners: Math • EMC 8254 • © Evan-Moor Corp.

School Days

Skill:
Measure length
in centimeters

This map represents the western half of the United States.

Use a centimeter ruler to measure distances to the nearest centimeter. Write the measurements. Then use them to answer the questions about distance.

Map Scale
1 cm = 250 km

1. Measure the distance from <u>Dallas</u>, Texas, to <u>Denver</u>, Colorado. About how many kilometers is it from <u>Dallas</u> to <u>Denver</u>?

   _____ cm   _____ km

2. Measure the distance from <u>Butte</u>, Montana, to <u>Dallas</u>, Texas. About how many kilometers is it from <u>Butte</u> to <u>Dallas</u>?

   _____ cm   _____ km

3. Measure the distance from <u>San Diego</u>, California, to <u>Boise</u>, Idaho. About how many kilometers is it from <u>San Diego</u> to <u>Boise</u>?

   _____ cm   _____ km

4. Measure the distance from <u>Phoenix</u>, Arizona, to <u>San Diego</u>, California. About how many kilometers is it from <u>Phoenix</u> to <u>San Diego</u>?

   _____ cm   _____ km

Add or subtract.

$$\begin{array}{r} 4,612 \\ + 3,209 \\ \hline \end{array} \qquad \begin{array}{r} 5,873 \\ + 2,456 \\ \hline \end{array} \qquad \begin{array}{r} 9,580 \\ - 3,177 \\ \hline \end{array} \qquad \begin{array}{r} 6,000 \\ - 1,248 \\ \hline \end{array}$$

Multiply or divide.

$$\begin{array}{r} 26 \\ \times \ 8 \\ \hline \end{array} \qquad \begin{array}{r} 53 \\ \times \ 7 \\ \hline \end{array} \qquad \begin{array}{r} 183 \\ \times \ 8 \\ \hline \end{array} \qquad \begin{array}{r} 3,272 \\ \times \ \ \ 5 \\ \hline \end{array}$$

$$4\overline{)72} \qquad 2\overline{)68} \qquad 5\overline{)850} \qquad 7\overline{)903}$$

Plot the fractions on the number line. Write **>**, **<**, or **=** to compare the fractions.

Draw a line of symmetry on the figure.

$\dfrac{3}{8}$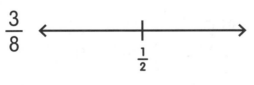

$\dfrac{3}{4}$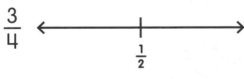

$\dfrac{3}{8} \bigcirc \dfrac{3}{4}$

Mia is 140 centimeters tall. Kasey is $1\frac{1}{2}$ meters tall. Who is taller? How many centimeters taller?

_____, _____ cm taller

Skill:
Write numbers
in standard form

Write each number in standard form.

1. There are more than nine hundred thousand different types of insects.

   _____

2. There are more beetles than any other kind of insect. More than three hundred fifty thousand types of beetles have been discovered.

   _____

3. There are about seventeen thousand five hundred types of butterflies laying eggs on plants.

   _____

4. More than twelve thousand different types of ants live in colonies around the world.

   _____

5. There are about twenty-five thousand types of bees pollinating plants.

   _____

6. Scientists have discovered more than one hundred sixty thousand types of flies.

   _____

7. There are more than five thousand types of dragonflies eating while in flight.

   _____

8. There are about eighteen thousand types of grasshoppers hopping around the world.

   _____

World of Insects

Leafy Numbers

Round each number to the place of the underlined digit.

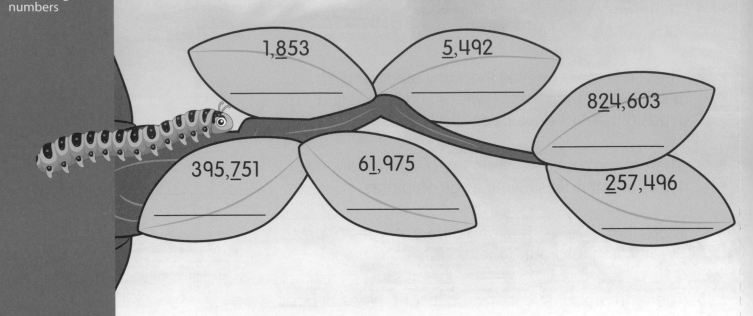

1,8<u>5</u>3 _____

<u>5</u>,492 _____

82<u>4</u>,603 _____

395,<u>7</u>51 _____

61,<u>9</u>75 _____

<u>2</u>57,496 _____

A scientist was counting caterpillars in four areas. Here are her results:

Area A	Area B	Area C	Area D
16,596	15,324	15,901	14,788

1. If the scientist rounded the numbers to the nearest ten, in which two areas would the tens digit **not** change? _____

2. If she rounded the numbers to the nearest hundred, in which two areas would the hundreds digit change? _____

3. If she rounded the numbers to the nearest thousand, in which area would the thousands digit **not** change? _____

4. If she rounded the numbers to the nearest thousand, which two areas would have the same number? _____

5. If the scientist rounded the numbers to the nearest ten thousand, which area would **not** have the same number as the others? _____

Skill Sharpeners: Math • EMC 8254 • © Evan-Moor Corp.

Making Large Numbers Simple

Round each number to the place value listed.

1. 7,465 (hundreds) _____

2. 14,309 (tens) _____

3. 28,731 (thousands) _____

4. 590,472 (ten thousands) _____

5. 289,962 (hundred thousands) _____

6. 190,749 (tens) _____

7. 83,802 (hundreds) _____

8. 730,801 (thousands) _____

9. 69,730 (ten thousands) _____

10. 287,521 (thousands) _____

Round the number **420,694** to the place values listed.

11. tens _____

12. hundreds _____

13. thousands _____

14. ten thousands _____

15. hundred thousands _____

World of Insects

Find the Factors

Factors are numbers that divide evenly into a given number. For example, the factors of **15** are **1, 3, 5,** and **15** because all of those numbers divide evenly into **15**.

Write all the factors of the following numbers.

 12 _____

 8 _____

 18 _____

 20 _____

 24 _____

30 _____

Skill Sharpeners: Math • EMC 8254 • © Evan-Moor Corp.

- Circle all prime numbers in red.
- Cross out all the composite numbers in blue.

The first prime number and the first composite number have been marked for you. The number **1** is blocked out because it is neither prime nor composite.

> **Prime numbers** have exactly two factors: **1** and the number itself.
> *Example: 2 (factors = 1 and 2)*
>
> **Composite numbers** have more than two factors. They are multiples of other numbers.
> *Example: 4 (factors = 1, 2, 4)*

Skill:
Identify prime and composite numbers

1	②	3	✗	5	6	7	8	9	10
11	12	13	14	15	16	17	18	19	20
21	22	23	24	25	26	27	28	29	30
31	32	33	34	35	36	37	38	39	40
41	42	43	44	45	46	47	48	49	50
51	52	53	54	55	56	57	58	59	60
61	62	63	64	65	66	67	68	69	70
71	72	73	74	75	76	77	78	79	80
81	82	83	84	85	86	87	88	89	90
91	92	93	94	95	96	97	98	99	100

World of Insects

Heading Home

Skill:
Identify prime and composite numbers

Help the bees reach their hive. Begin at **Start**. Stop at each circled number. Decide if it is prime (**P**) or composite (**C**) and take the path that matches. Then continue until you reach the hive.

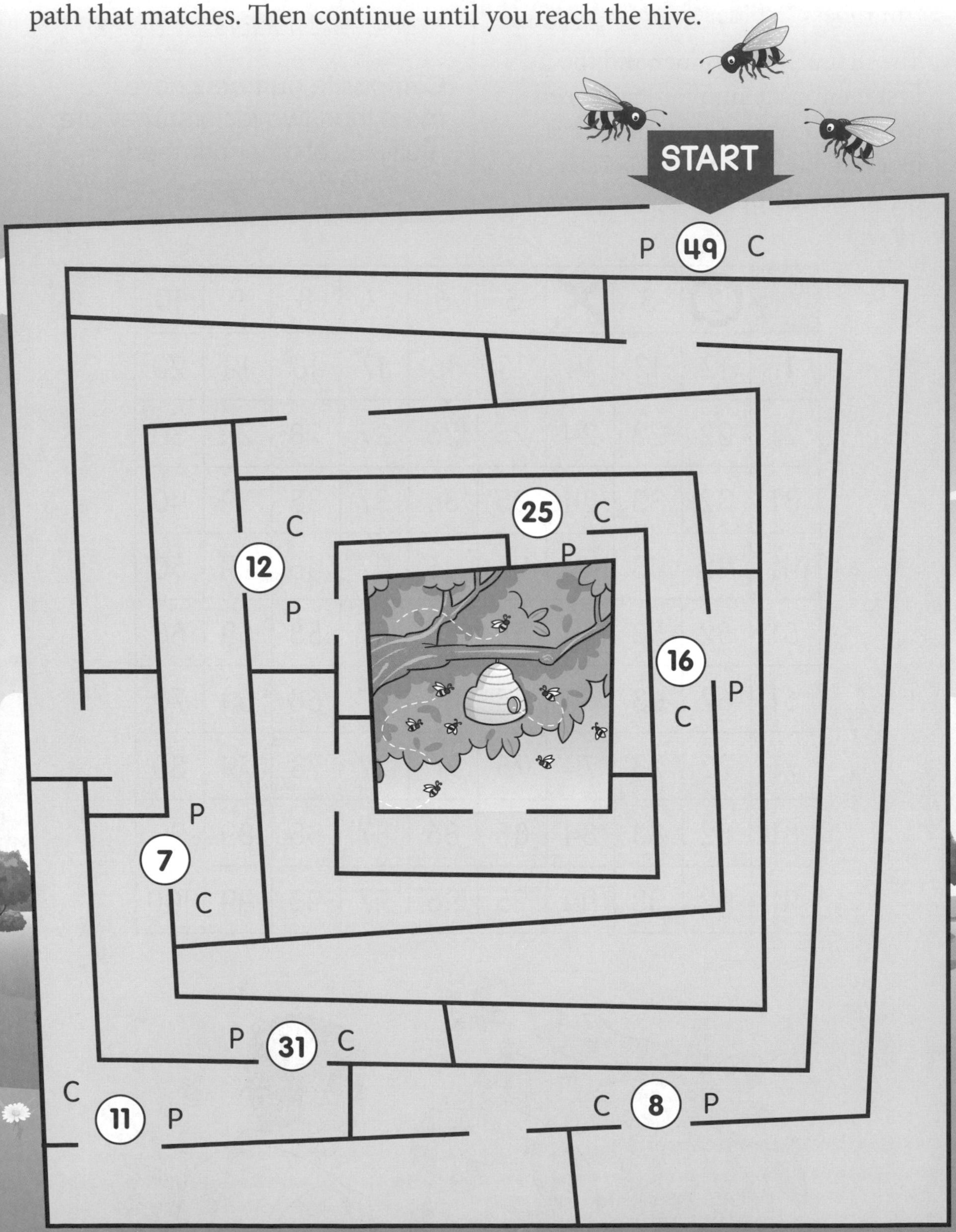
START
P 49 C
C 12 P
25 C P
16 P C
P 7 C
P 31 C
C 11 P
C 8 P

World of Insects

Skill:
Add fractions and mixed numbers

> ## What is the world's largest ant?

To find the answer to the riddle, first solve the problems below.
Then write the matching letter at the bottom of the page.

A $1\frac{1}{4} + \frac{2}{4} =$ ___ $1\frac{3}{4}$

O $2\frac{1}{8} + 2\frac{4}{8} =$ ___

C $\frac{1}{4} + \frac{3}{4} =$ ___

P $\frac{2}{7} + 1\frac{2}{7} =$ ___

E $\frac{1}{8} + \frac{6}{8} =$ ___

R $\frac{1}{9} + \frac{4}{9} =$ ___

F $1\frac{1}{3} + 1\frac{1}{3} =$ ___

S $\frac{4}{7} + 1\frac{1}{7} =$ ___

H $\frac{2}{5} + \frac{2}{5} =$ ___

T $2\frac{1}{5} + 1\frac{2}{5} =$ ___

L $\frac{1}{7} + \frac{4}{7} =$ ___

U $1\frac{2}{4} + 1\frac{1}{4} =$ ___

N $\frac{1}{9} + \frac{7}{9} =$ ___

A	
$1\frac{3}{4}$	$\frac{8}{9}$

$\frac{7}{8}$	$\frac{5}{7}$	$\frac{7}{8}$	$1\frac{4}{7}$	$\frac{4}{5}$	$1\frac{3}{4}$	$\frac{8}{9}$	$3\frac{3}{5}$

,

$4\frac{5}{8}$	$2\frac{2}{3}$	1	$4\frac{5}{8}$	$2\frac{3}{4}$	$\frac{5}{9}$	$1\frac{5}{7}$	$\frac{7}{8}$

!

World of Insects

Bee Careful!

Solve the problems.

1. $\frac{2}{3} - \frac{1}{3} = $ _____

2. $\frac{6}{7} - \frac{1}{7} = $ _____

3. $\frac{3}{4} - \frac{2}{4} = $ _____

4. $\frac{8}{9} - \frac{1}{9} = $ _____

5. $\frac{4}{5} - \frac{2}{5} = $ _____

6. $\frac{6}{7} - \frac{3}{7} = $ _____

7. $\frac{7}{8} - \frac{6}{8} = $ _____

8. $\frac{5}{6} - \frac{4}{6} = $ _____

9. $\frac{9}{10} - \frac{2}{10} = $ _____

10. $\frac{8}{9} - \frac{6}{9} = $ _____

11. $6\frac{3}{4} - 1\frac{1}{4} = $ _____

12. $5\frac{4}{9} - 1\frac{2}{9} = $ _____

13. $6\frac{6}{7} - 2\frac{1}{7} = $ _____

14. $5\frac{4}{5} - 2\frac{1}{5} = $ _____

15. $8\frac{7}{8} - 5\frac{6}{8} = $ _____

16. $4\frac{9}{10} - 2\frac{6}{10} = $ _____

$\frac{5}{8} - \frac{2}{8} = \frac{3}{8}$

World of Insects

A Bug's Rugs

This bug loves rugs! Use the clues to figure out the length or width of each rug in the bug's collection.

Skills:
Determine area and perimeter; Solve word problems

1. The area is 12 square feet. The length is 4 feet. What is the width?

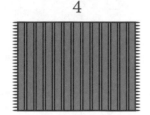

_____ feet

2. The perimeter is 12 feet. The width is 2 feet. What is the length?

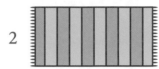

_____ feet

3. The area of the square rug is 9 square feet. What is the length of each side?

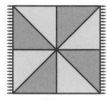

_____ feet

4. The perimeter of the square rug is 28 feet. What is the length of each side?

_____ feet

5. The area is 24 square feet. The perimeter is 20 feet. What are the length and width?

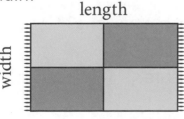

length _____ feet

width _____ feet

6. The area is 15 square feet. The perimeter is 16 feet. What are the length and width?

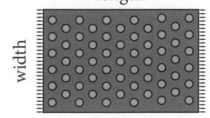

length _____ feet

width _____ feet

World of Insects

Insect Lengths

Skill:
Interpret a line plot

A scientist observed some insects and measured their lengths. He recorded the results on a line plot. Use it to answer the questions.

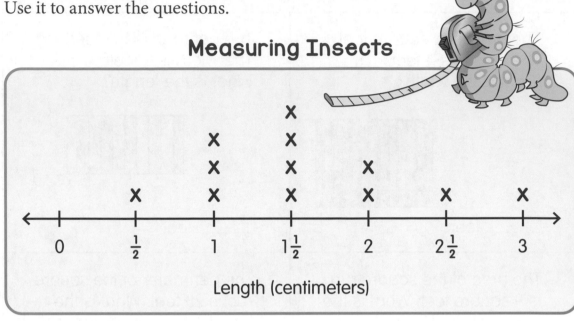

Measuring Insects

Length (centimeters)

1. How long was the shortest insect? _____ cm

2. How long was the longest insect? _____ cm

3. How much longer was the longest insect than the shortest one? _____ cm

4. How many insects were at least $1\frac{1}{2}$ centimeters long? _____ insects

5. How many insects were less than 2 centimeters long? _____ insects

6. How many insects did the scientist measure? _____ insects

7. Which length was the most common? _____ cm

8. If all the insects were lined up end to end, how long a line would they form? _____ cm

Skill Sharpeners: Math • EMC 8254 • © Evan-Moor Corp.

Butterfly Symmetry

Butterflies have a symmetrical shape and pattern.
Each half of the butterfly matches the other.
Draw the missing half of each butterfly and color it.
For the last two butterflies, draw your own amazing patterns!

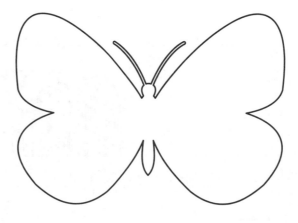

World of Insects

Round each number to the underlined digit.

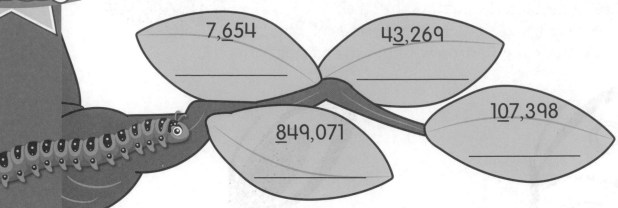

7,654

_____

43,269

_____

849,071

_____

107,398

_____

Write all the factors of these numbers.

16 _____

21 _____

Write **P** or **C** to show if the number is prime or composite.

5 _____   27 _____

9 _____   13 _____

Add or subtract.

$\frac{1}{2} + \frac{1}{2} =$ _____

$\frac{1}{4} + \frac{2}{4} =$ _____

$\frac{1}{8} + \frac{2}{8} =$ _____

$\frac{5}{6} - \frac{4}{6} =$ _____

$\frac{9}{10} - \frac{2}{10} =$ _____

$\frac{4}{5} - \frac{2}{5} =$ _____

$1\frac{1}{9} + 7\frac{3}{9} =$ _____

$6\frac{5}{7} - 3\frac{3}{7} =$ _____

$3\frac{1}{2} - 1\frac{1}{2} =$ _____

Solve each problem.

The area of a rectangular rug is 24 square feet. Its length is 6 feet. What is its width?

_____ feet

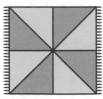

The perimeter of a square rug is 20 feet. What is the length of each side?

_____ feet

Skill:
Use logical thinking

Each cookie below represents a number: **1, 2, 3, 4, 6, 8**.
Use the equations to determine the value of each cookie.
Write the values of the cookies at the bottom of the page.

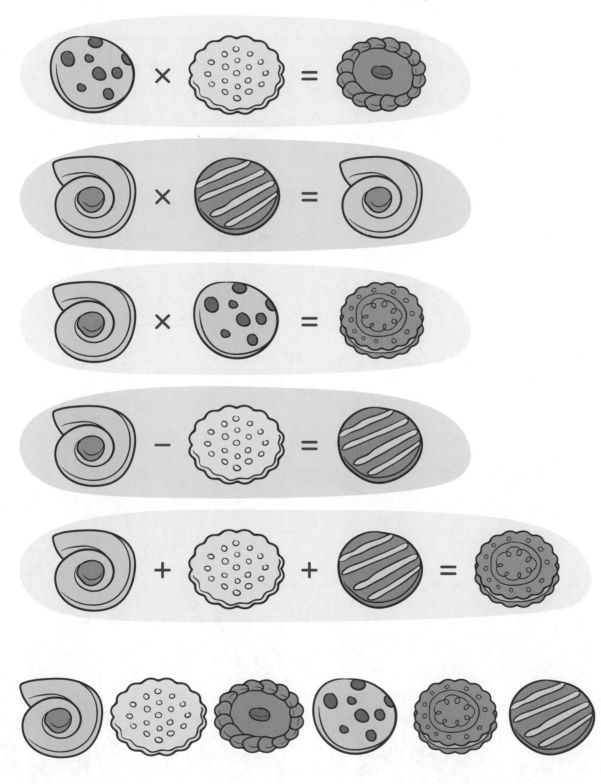

At the Bakery

____ ____ ____ ____ ____ ____

Best-Selling Bread

Skill:
Multiply with
multiples of 10

Big Bread Bakery makes delicious bread! Find out which one is its best seller. First, multiply and write the answers. Then use the key to write the matching letters in the order of the problems on the bottom of the page.

400 **R**	1,000 **E**	1,500 **N**	2,400 **A**
800 **I**	1,200 **A**	1,600 **B**	4,200 **I**
900 **S**	1,400 **R**	2,100 **D**	

1. 20 × 20 = _____

2. 30 × 40 = _____

3. 60 × 70 = _____

4. 30 × 30 = _____

5. 20 × 40 = _____

6. 50 × 30 = _____

7. 40 × 40 = _____

8. 70 × 20 = _____

9. 20 × 50 = _____

10. 60 × 40 = _____

11. 30 × 70 = _____

What is Big Bread Bakery's best-selling bread?

_____ _____ _____ _____ _____ _____

_____ _____ _____ _____ _____

At the Bakery

Multiply.

$$\begin{array}{r} 24 \\ \times\ 20 \\ \hline \end{array}$$

$$\begin{array}{r} 13 \\ \times\ 30 \\ \hline \end{array}$$

$$\begin{array}{r} 31 \\ \times\ 50 \\ \hline \end{array}$$

$$\begin{array}{r} 42 \\ \times\ 40 \\ \hline \end{array}$$

$$\begin{array}{r} 93 \\ \times\ 40 \\ \hline \end{array}$$

$$\begin{array}{r} 68 \\ \times\ 20 \\ \hline \end{array}$$

$$\begin{array}{r} 19 \\ \times\ 70 \\ \hline \end{array}$$

$$\begin{array}{r} 36 \\ \times\ 40 \\ \hline \end{array}$$

$$\begin{array}{r} 57 \\ \times\ 60 \\ \hline \end{array}$$

$$\begin{array}{r} 91 \\ \times\ 90 \\ \hline \end{array}$$

$$\begin{array}{r} 83 \\ \times\ 30 \\ \hline \end{array}$$

$$\begin{array}{r} 65 \\ \times\ 50 \\ \hline \end{array}$$

How will knowing **62 × 3** help you solve **62 × 30**?

_____

_____

_____

_____

_____

_____

At the Bakery

Bakery Buys

Skill:
Solve word problems

Solve the problems.

A Girl Scout leader buys 16 bagels for her troop every week. How many bagels will she have bought after 5 weeks?

_____ bagels

Bob's Bakery sold 15 dozen cookies a day. How many cookies was that? (A dozen is a group of 12.)

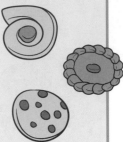

_____ cookies

Bob's Bakery sold 9 cherry pies on Friday for $108. How much did each pie cost?

$_____

Eight boxes of donuts were sold. There were 16 donuts in each box. How many donuts were sold?

_____ donuts

Bob's Bakery sold 360 muffins in 4 days. He sold the same number each day. How many muffins were sold each day?

_____ muffins

Bob's Bakery sells pie by the slice. Each pie is cut into 8 slices. Last weekend, 280 slices were sold. How many whole pies did Bob start with?

_____

At the Bakery

Skill Sharpeners: Math • EMC 8254 • © Evan-Moor Corp.

Skill:
Find multiples

Multiples are the product of a whole number and any other given number. For example, the first five multiples of **7** are **7**, **14**, **21**, **28**, and **35**. These numbers come from the following products:

$$7 \times 1 = 7 \qquad 7 \times 4 = 28$$
$$7 \times 2 = 14 \qquad 7 \times 5 = 35$$
$$7 \times 3 = 21$$

What are the first five multiples for each of the following numbers?

A+ the Bakery

© Evan-Moor Corp. • EMC 8254 • Skill Sharpeners: Math

47

A Grand Opening

A bakery served pies at its grand opening. All the pies were the same size. Here are three pies that were served. Write a fraction to show how much of each pie was left.

Pie A 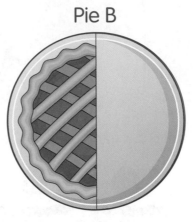 Pie B Pie C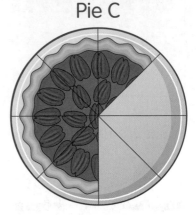

_____   _____   _____

Which pie had the largest amount left? _____

Which pie had the smallest amount left? _____

The bakery also served 3 large cakes. After two hours, the baker saw how much of each cake was left: $\frac{1}{3}$ of cake A, $\frac{1}{6}$ of cake B, and $\frac{5}{12}$ of cake C. Draw pictures to show how much of each cake was left.

Cake A	Cake B	Cake C
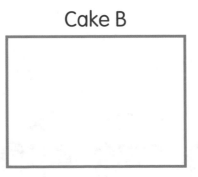		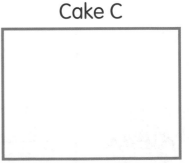

List the fractions in order from the smallest to the largest.   _____, _____, _____

Skill Sharpeners: Math • EMC 8254 • © Evan-Moor Corp.

At the Bakery

Skill:

Multiply a whole number by a fraction

Solve the problems. Write your answers as whole numbers or mixed numbers.

1. A baker made 7 batches of cookies. She used $\frac{1}{2}$ teaspoon of salt for each batch. How many teaspoons of salt did she use in all?

$$7 \times \frac{1}{2} = \frac{7}{2}$$
$$= 3\frac{1}{2}$$

$3\frac{1}{2}$ teaspoons

2. A brownie recipe calls for $\frac{3}{4}$ cup of flour. The recipe makes 16 brownies. How much flour is needed for 48 brownies?

_____ cups

3. It takes $\frac{1}{3}$ cup of sour cream to make 1 loaf of lemon bread. A baker made 6 loaves of lemon bread. How many cups of sour cream did he use?

_____ cups

4. It takes $\frac{1}{4}$ cup of butter to make 1 batch of biscuits. How many cups of butter are needed for 5 batches?

_____ cups

5. An apple pie recipe calls for $\frac{1}{8}$ teaspoon of nutmeg. How much nutmeg is needed for 15 apple pies?

_____ teaspoons

Cake Candles

Write the rule for each pattern. Then write the next number in the pattern.

1.     2 5 8 11 ___14___

   What's the rule? _____Start with 2. Add 3._____

2.    1 3 5 7 _____

   What's the rule? _____

3.     1 6 11 16 _____

   What's the rule? _____

4.    2 4 8 16 _____

   What's the rule? _____

Cool Cupcakes

Every day, a bakery displayed cupcakes in long rows.
Read the clues and answer the questions.

1. On Monday, there were 24 cupcakes.
Every 2nd cupcake was purple.
Every 3rd cupcake had sprinkles.

   How many cupcakes were purple? _____

   How many cupcakes had sprinkles? _____

   How many cupcakes were purple **and** had sprinkles? _____

2. On Tuesday, there were 40 cupcakes.
Every 4th cupcake had vanilla icing.
Every 5th cupcake had a cherry on top.

   How many cupcakes had vanilla icing? _____

   How many cupcakes had a cherry on top? _____

   How many cupcakes had vanilla icing **and** a cherry? _____

3. On Wednesday, there were 36 cupcakes.
Every 3rd cupcake was chocolate. Every
6th cupcake had candy stars.

   How many cupcakes were chocolate? _____

   How many cupcakes had candy stars? _____

   How many chocolate cupcakes **also** had candy stars? _____

At the Bakery

51

Bakery Weights

Use the information in the box to help you solve the problems.

> ## U.S. Customary Units of Weight
> 16 ounces (oz.) = 1 pound (lb.)

1. A baker used 5 pounds of flour to make several loaves of bread. How many ounces of flour did the baker use?

   _____ oz.

2. A cake weighed 48 ounces. How many pounds did it weigh?

   _____ lb.

3. Which weighs more—30 ounces of white sugar or 2 pounds of brown sugar? How much more?

   _____, _____ oz. more

4. A loaf of bread weighed 24 ounces. Is that greater than, less than, or equal to $1\frac{1}{2}$ pounds?

   _____

5. An 8-ounce bag of pretzel sticks sells for $2.00. How much would $1\frac{1}{2}$ pounds of pretzel sticks cost?

   $_____

6. A large cake weighed 20 pounds and served 100 people. How many pounds would half the cake weigh?

   _____ lb.

   How many ounces is that?

   _____ oz.

At the Bakery

Perfect Pies Bakery sells different pies for different prices. Read the clues and fill in the table to match each pie with its price. When you know that a pie and a price do **not** go together, make an **X** under that price and across from that pie. When you know that a pie and a price **do** go together, write **YES** in that box.

Skill:
Use logical thinking

Clues

- The apple pie is not the most expensive pie.
- The lemon pie costs more than the cherry pie.
- The blueberry pie costs more than $12.
- The strawberry pie costs more than the blueberry pie.
- The cherry pie is not the least expensive pie.

	$8	$10	$12	$14	$16
apple					
blueberry					
strawberry					
lemon					
cherry					

Write the price beside the matching pie.

apple $_____

blueberry $_____

strawberry $_____

lemon $_____

cherry $_____

At the Bakery

Watch the Time!

Solve the problems.

1. A baker put a loaf of pumpkin bread into the oven at 1:20 p.m. It needs to bake for 70 minutes.

   At what time should the baker take the loaf out of the oven? Write the time and show your answer on the clock.

   _____

2. A baker was making 3 batches of sugar cookies. It took only 8 minutes to bake one batch. The baker put the first batch in the oven at 9:45 a.m.

   At what time did the baker take out the last batch?

   _____

3. A baker started making apple cake at 8:30 a.m. She spent 10 minutes preparing the batter. Then she baked the cake for 65 minutes.

   At what time was the cake done? Write the time and show your answer on the clock.

   _____

4. A baker put bread in the oven at 6:42 a.m. The bread needs to bake for 50 minutes. It is 7:05 a.m.

   How much longer does the bread need to bake?

   _____ more minutes

At the Bakery

Multiply.

$$31 \times 20$$ $$24 \times 40$$ $$56 \times 30$$ $$72 \times 50$$

Write the first three multiples of these numbers.

2 _____   3 _____

5 _____   9 _____

Solve. Write your answers as whole numbers or mixed numbers.

A baker made 5 batches of brownies. He used $\frac{3}{4}$ cup of flour for each batch. How much flour did he use?

_____ cups

It takes $\frac{1}{4}$ cup of butter to make 1 batch of biscuits. How many cups of butter are needed for 8 batches?

_____ cups

Solve.

3 pounds = _____ ounces

32 ounces = _____ pounds

$1\frac{1}{2}$ pounds = _____ ounces

40 ounces = _____ pounds

Solve.

A baker made 3 batches of cookies. Each batch took 12 minutes to bake. The first batch went into the oven at 12:45 p.m. At what time did the last batch come out of the oven?

_____

At the Bakery

A Chilly Puzzle

Draw a straight line connecting each number with its word form.

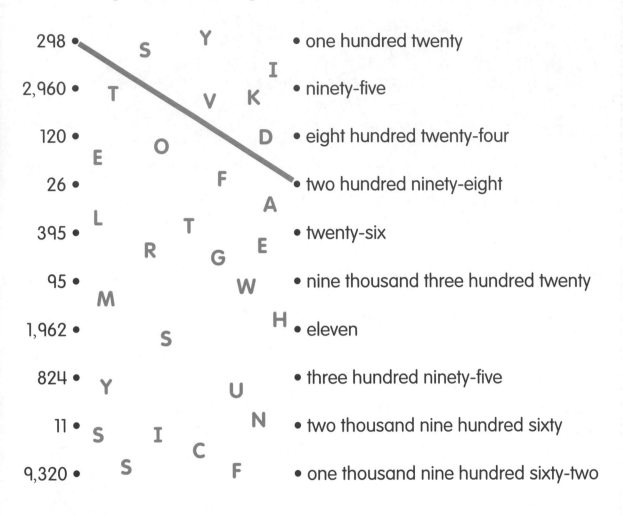

298 •   S   Y   I   • one hundred twenty

2,960 •   T   V   K   • ninety-five

120 •   O   D • eight hundred twenty-four

   E

26 •   F   • two hundred ninety-eight

    A

395 •   L   T   E • twenty-six

   R   G

95 •   W   • nine thousand three hundred twenty

  M

     H

1,962 •   S   • eleven

824 •   Y   U   • three hundred ninety-five

     N

11 • S   I   • two thousand nine hundred sixty

     C

9,320 •   S   F • one thousand nine hundred sixty-two

Look at the letters that are inside the five polygons formed by the lines you drew above. Arrange the letters to spell the name of something that you might see on a cold winter day.

_____ _____ _____ _____ _____

Hint

A **polygon** is a closed figure made with straight sides.

polygon   not a polygon

A Snowy Hill

Multiply.

Skill:

Multiply
multidigit
numbers

$$\begin{array}{r} 43 \\ \times\ 21 \\ \hline \end{array}$$
$$\begin{array}{r} 32 \\ \times\ 23 \\ \hline \end{array}$$
$$\begin{array}{r} 27 \\ \times\ 34 \\ \hline \end{array}$$
$$\begin{array}{r} 25 \\ \times\ 25 \\ \hline \end{array}$$

$$\begin{array}{r} 17 \\ \times\ 16 \\ \hline \end{array}$$
$$\begin{array}{r} 23 \\ \times\ 42 \\ \hline \end{array}$$
$$\begin{array}{r} 39 \\ \times\ 31 \\ \hline \end{array}$$
$$\begin{array}{r} 62 \\ \times\ 25 \\ \hline \end{array}$$

$$\begin{array}{r} 57 \\ \times\ 52 \\ \hline \end{array}$$
$$\begin{array}{r} 82 \\ \times\ 24 \\ \hline \end{array}$$
$$\begin{array}{r} 76 \\ \times\ 37 \\ \hline \end{array}$$
$$\begin{array}{r} 94 \\ \times\ 42 \\ \hline \end{array}$$

$$\begin{array}{r} 37 \\ \times\ 47 \\ \hline \end{array}$$
$$\begin{array}{r} 78 \\ \times\ 59 \\ \hline \end{array}$$
$$\begin{array}{r} 65 \\ \times\ 47 \\ \hline \end{array}$$

Winter Fun

A Winter Tongue Twister

Solve the division problems. Then write the letter from the code for each remainder to make a tongue twister. Try saying the phrase quickly three times!

Remainder Code

1	**E**	5	**O**
2	**I**	6	**S**
3	**M**	7	**W**
4	**N**	8	**X**

$34 \div 7 = \underline{\ \ 4\ \ }$ remainder of $\underline{\ \ 6\ \ }$ $\underline{\ \ S\ \ }$

$20 \div 6 = \underline{\hspace{1cm}}$ remainder of $\underline{\hspace{1cm}}$ $\underline{\hspace{1cm}}$

$80 \div 9 = \underline{\hspace{1cm}}$ remainder of $\underline{\hspace{1cm}}$ $\underline{\hspace{1cm}}$

$54 \div 8 = \underline{\hspace{1cm}}$ remainder of $\underline{\hspace{1cm}}$ $\underline{\hspace{1cm}}$

$49 \div 5 = \underline{\hspace{1cm}}$ remainder of $\underline{\hspace{1cm}}$ $\underline{\hspace{1cm}}$

$35 \div 6 = \underline{\hspace{1cm}}$ remainder of $\underline{\hspace{1cm}}$ $\underline{\hspace{1cm}}$

$43 \div 9 = \underline{\hspace{1cm}}$ remainder of $\underline{\hspace{1cm}}$ $\underline{\hspace{1cm}}$

$39 \div 4 = \underline{\hspace{1cm}}$ remainder of $\underline{\hspace{1cm}}$ $\underline{\hspace{1cm}}$

$50 \div 7 = \underline{\hspace{1cm}}$ remainder of $\underline{\hspace{1cm}}$ $\underline{\hspace{1cm}}$

$68 \div 8 = \underline{\hspace{1cm}}$ remainder of $\underline{\hspace{1cm}}$ $\underline{\hspace{1cm}}$

Skill:
Divide with remainders

Solve the division problems.

$$\begin{array}{r} 10\ R2 \\ 4\overline{)42} \\ -40 \\ \hline 2 \end{array}$$

$6\overline{)59}$

$3\overline{)28}$

$9\overline{)75}$

$7\overline{)83}$

$5\overline{)93}$

$4\overline{)87}$

$3\overline{)98}$

$2\overline{)249}$

$4\overline{)893}$

$3\overline{)986}$

$5\overline{)674}$

Winter Fun

Winter Activities

Skill:
Solve word problems

Solve the problems.

A group of 35 people are going snowboarding. Everyone will travel by van. If each van holds 8 people, how many vans are needed? Explain.

_____

_____

_____

_____

Caleb collected 40 pinecones for a craft project. He put them in bowls. If each bowl held 12 pinecones, how many did **not** fit in the bowls? Explain.

_____

_____

_____

_____

There are 52 people taking skiing lessons. Each full class has 9 students. Every class is full except for one. How many full classes are there? Explain.

_____

_____

Reni had $100 to spend going skiing. It was enough money to ski for 6 days. Each day, she had to buy a ticket to go up the snowy mountain. How much did it cost each day to ski? Explain.

_____

_____

Winter Fun

Skill:
Estimate weight, length, capacity, and time

Circle the best estimate for each question.

About how heavy is a pair of children's boots?

a. 1 gram

b. 1 kilogram

c. 1 milligram

About how much does a bucket hold?

a. 5 centiliters

b. 5 milliliters

c. 5 liters

About how heavy is an ice cube?

a. 30 milligrams

b. 30 kilograms

c. 30 grams

About how much does a soupspoon hold?

a. 9 liters

b. 9 milliliters

c. 9 centiliters

About how far is it from the floor to the ceiling?

a. 2 meters

b. 2 centimeters

c. 2 kilometers

About how long does it take to brush your teeth?

a. 2 hours

b. 2 seconds

c. 2 minutes

About how long is a new pencil?

a. 20 millimeters

b. 20 centimeters

c. 20 meters

About how long does it take to walk up a staircase?

a. 15 seconds

b. 15 minutes

c. 15 hours

Winter Fun

Wintry Places

Use the map scale and a centimeter ruler to estimate the following distances in kilometers. Measure from the center of the orange squares to determine the distances.

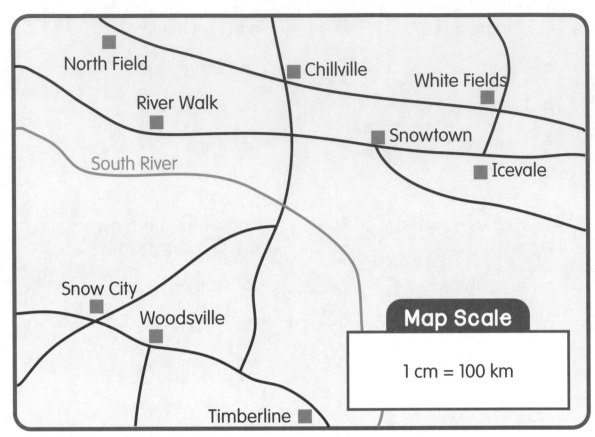

1. About how far apart are North Field and River Walk? _____ km

2. About how many kilometers is it between Snow City and Snowtown? _____ km

3. About how far is it from Woodsville to Timberline? _____ km

4. About how many kilometers is it between Woodsville and White Fields? _____ km

5. About how far is it from Icevale to Chillville? _____ km

6. About how far apart are White Fields and North Field? _____ km

Skill:
Write tenths as fractions and decimals

Quinn made some quilts. She kept track of her quilt patterns by recording the colors as fractions and decimals.

Write a fraction and a decimal to describe the quilt colors below.

Four tenths of the quilt is yellow and six tenths is blue.

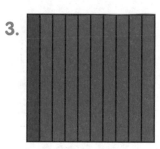

yellow	$\frac{4}{10}$	0.4
blue	$\frac{6}{10}$	0.6

1.

orange _____

purple _____

2.

green _____

yellow _____

3.

red _____

blue _____

4.

green _____

blue _____

purple _____

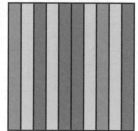

5.

green _____

yellow _____

orange _____

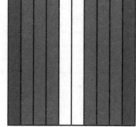

6.

red _____

blue _____

white _____

Winter Fun

Totally Cool!

Write a fraction and a decimal to describe what part of each square
is colored.

1.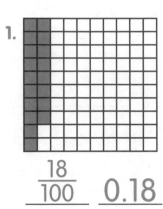

$$\frac{18}{100} \quad 0.18$$

2.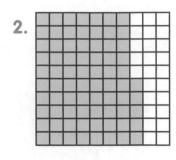

_____ _____

3.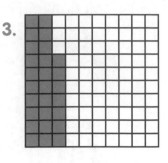

_____ _____

4.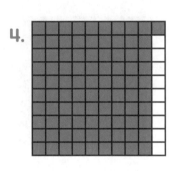

5.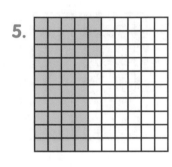

6.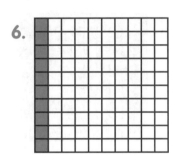

_____ _____

7.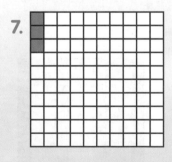

8.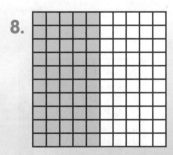

9.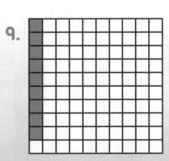

_____ _____

Lines, Line Segments, and Rays

A **line** goes in opposite directions without ending.

A **line segment** is part of a line. It has two endpoints.

A **ray** is part of a line that goes in one direction without ending. It has one endpoint.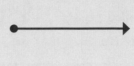

Write the name for each figure.

1.

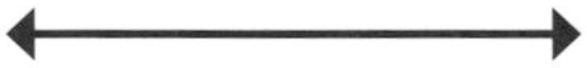

___line___

2.

_____

3. 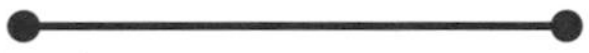 ●————————●

_____

4.

_____

5.

_____

6.

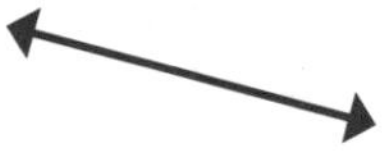

_____

Draw.

line segment	ray	line

Winter Fun

Skating Time

Write **intersecting**, **parallel**, or **perpendicular** to describe each pair of lines.

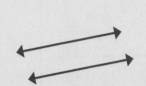 **Parallel** lines never meet.

 **Intersecting** lines meet or cross.

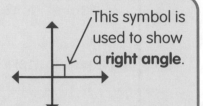 This symbol is used to show a **right angle**.

Perpendicular lines meet at right angles.

1.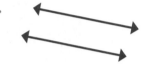

_____

2.

_____

3.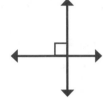

_____

4.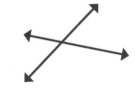

_____

5.

_____

6.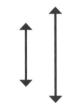

_____

7. Are perpendicular lines always intersecting lines? _____

8. Are intersecting lines always perpendicular lines? _____

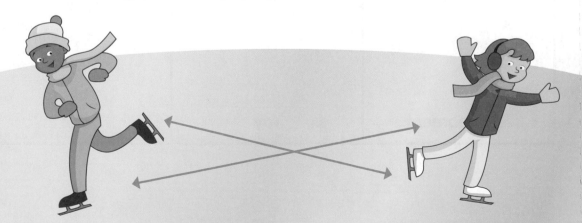

Winter Fun

Write the matching numbers.

ninety thousand ninety-nine _____

nine hundred nine thousand nine _____

nine thousand nine hundred ninety _____

Which number is the largest? _____

Which number is the smallest? _____

Multiply.

$$\begin{array}{r} 27 \\ \times\ 35 \\ \hline \end{array} \qquad \begin{array}{r} 62 \\ \times\ 49 \\ \hline \end{array}$$

Divide.

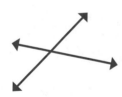 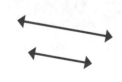

Write a fraction and a decimal for the blue part.

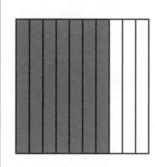 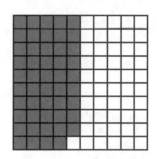

_____ _____ _____   _____ _____ _____

Write **intersecting**, **parallel**, or **perpendicular** to describe the lines.

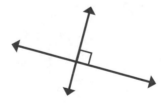

_____   _____   _____

Use the centimeter ruler to answer the question.

How far is it from Point B to Point C? _____ cm

Name the Pet

Skill:
Round large
numbers

Match each pet with its bowl. Use the number **9,369,639,201**
to help you. Each bowl has a rounded form of the number.
Draw a line connecting each rounded number to the place
value that the original number was rounded to.

Fido
9,400,000,000 •

• ten millions

Curly
9,000,000,000 •

• hundred thousands

Rascal
9,369,640,000 •

• hundred millions

Tom
9,370,000,000 •

• billions

Dipsey
9,369,639,200 •

• ten thousands

Smiley
9,369,600,000 •

• tens

Pet Pals

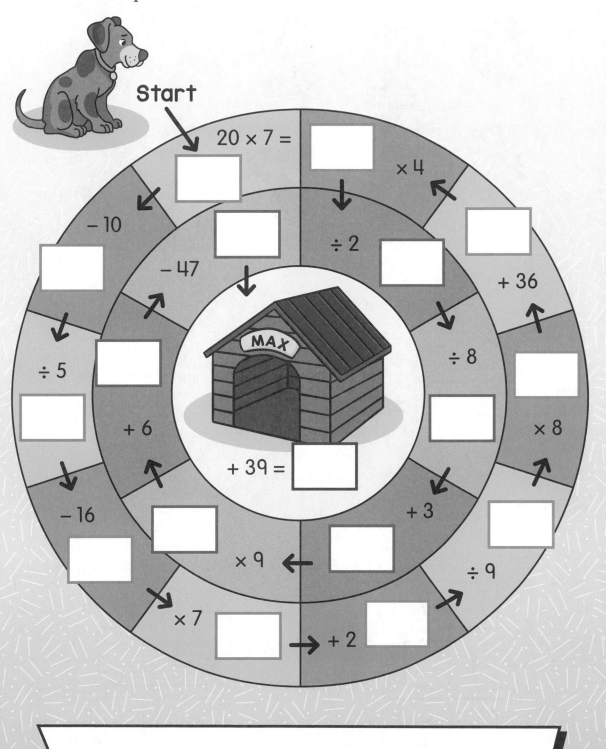

The Trail Home

Help Max find his way home. Start by solving the problem next to Max. Follow the arrows, using the previous answer to start the next problem.

Skill:
Add, subtract, multiply, and divide within 1,000

Start

$20 \times 7 =$

$\times 4$

$\div 2$

-10

-47

$+ 36$

$\div 5$

MAX

$\div 8$

$+ 6$

$+ 39 =$

$\times 8$

-16

$+ 3$

$\times 9$

$\div 9$

$\times 7$

$+ 2$

Pet Pals

What is the number you wrote on the doghouse? _____

Use the digits **0** to **9** to complete the operations.
Use each number only once.

$$2\boxed{} \div \boxed{} = \boxed{}$$

$$\begin{array}{r} 7 \\ \times\ \boxed{} \\ \hline 56 \end{array}$$

$$\begin{array}{r} \boxed{}\ 7 \\ -\ 1\ \boxed{} \\ \hline \boxed{}\ 1 \end{array}$$

$$\begin{array}{r} 1\ 6 \\ +\ 3\ \boxed{} \\ \hline \boxed{}\ \boxed{} \end{array}$$

Skill Sharpeners: Math • EMC 8254 • © Evan-Moor Corp.

Color to match the decimals. Then write **>**, **<** , or **=** in the circles to compare the decimals in each pair.

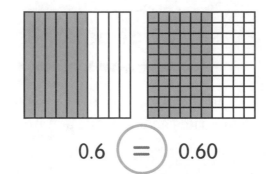

0.6 (**=**) 0.60

Skill:
Compare decimals

1.

0.7 ◯ 0.5

2.

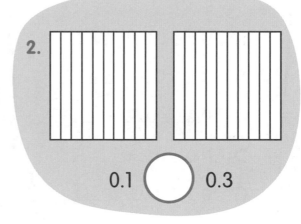

0.1 ◯ 0.3

3.

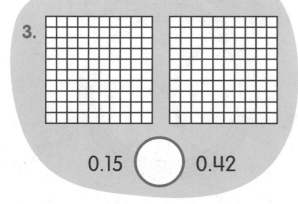

0.15 ◯ 0.42

4.

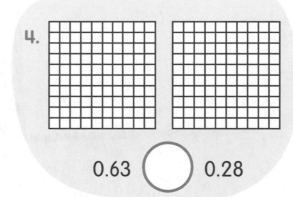

0.63 ◯ 0.28

5.

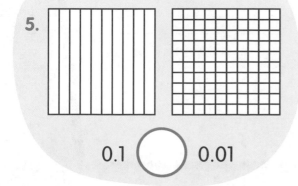

0.1 ◯ 0.01

6.

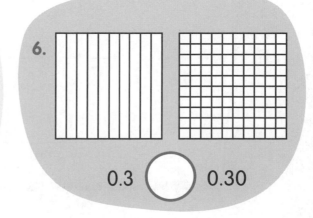

0.3 ◯ 0.30

Pet Pals

A Funny Pet Riddle

What pet goes ticktock, woof woof?

To find the answer to the riddle, first solve each problem.
Then write the letter on each line above the matching sum.

A   0.5 + 0.3 = _____

A   0.4 + 0.2 = _____

C   0.25 + 0.52 = _____

D   4.0 + 0.2 = _____

G   0.5 + 3.0 = _____

H   0.3 + 0.27 = _____

O   2.5 + 0.52 = _____

T   0.25 + 5.2 = _____

W   0.52 + 0.71 = _____

_____   _____   _____   _____   _____   _____
0.6   1.23   0.8   5.45   0.77   0.57

_____   _____   _____
4.2   3.02   3.5

Pet Pals

Skill:
Subtract decimals

Solve the problems. Then write the letter for each answer on the matching line below. Try saying the tongue twister quickly three times!

A $\begin{array}{r} 2.5 \\ -1.2 \\ \hline \end{array}$

D $\begin{array}{r} 5.3 \\ -2.1 \\ \hline \end{array}$

E $\begin{array}{r} 4.6 \\ -1.3 \\ \hline \end{array}$

H $\begin{array}{r} 9.5 \\ -8.4 \\ \hline \end{array}$

I $\begin{array}{r} 5.2 \\ -4.8 \\ \hline \end{array}$

K $\begin{array}{r} 4.12 \\ -3.09 \\ \hline \end{array}$

L $\begin{array}{r} 5.26 \\ -4.13 \\ \hline \end{array}$

N $\begin{array}{r} 8.69 \\ -1.26 \\ \hline \end{array}$

R $\begin{array}{r} 6.49 \\ -5.2 \\ \hline \end{array}$

S $\begin{array}{r} 7.25 \\ -4.1 \\ \hline \end{array}$

T $\begin{array}{r} 5.5 \\ -1.26 \\ \hline \end{array}$

V $\begin{array}{r} 8.24 \\ -7.03 \\ \hline \end{array}$

Y $\begin{array}{r} 4.81 \\ -3.07 \\ \hline \end{array}$

___	___	___	___	___	___	___	___	___	___
3.15	3.3	1.21	3.3	7.43	3.15	0.4	1.13	1.13	1.74

___	___	___	___	___	___
3.15	7.43	1.3	1.03	3.3	3.15

___	___	___	___	___	___	___	___	___
3.15	1.13	0.4	4.24	1.1	3.3	1.29	3.3	3.2

Pet Pals

At the Pet Store

Skills:
Solve word problems; Add and subtract decimals

Solve the problems.

Amir went to the pet store to buy birdseed. The food cost $2.94. Amir paid with a $5.00 bill. How much change did he get back?

$_____

Kiana bought her dog a leash and a collar. The leash cost $4.75 and the collar cost $6.50. Kiana paid with a $20.00 bill. How much change did she get back?

$_____

A neon tetra is a small aquarium fish. One store is selling them for $1.60 each. If Seth has a $10.00 bill, how many neon tetras can he buy?

_____ fish

Lara bought the wrong kind of turtle food. The store gives her a refund of $5.70. The new food that she buys costs $10.25. She uses her refund to pay for part of the new food. How much more does she need to pay?

$_____

Toshi will buy 3 cat toys for $1.92 each. If he pays in dollar bills, how many will he need?

_____ dollar bills

How much change will he receive? $_____

Skill Sharpeners: Math • EMC 8254 • © Evan-Moor Corp.

Pet Pals

Shape Patterns

Skill:
Analyze and extend patterns

Draw the next three figures in each pattern.
Write a rule for each pattern.

1.

rule: ____________________

2.

rule: ____________________

3.

rule: ____________________

4.

rule: ____________________

5.

rule: ____________________

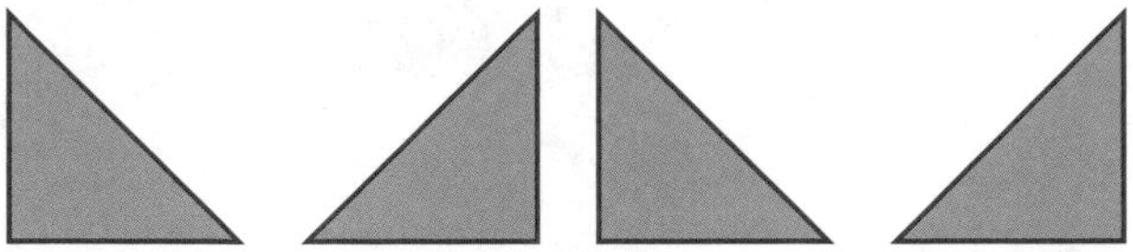

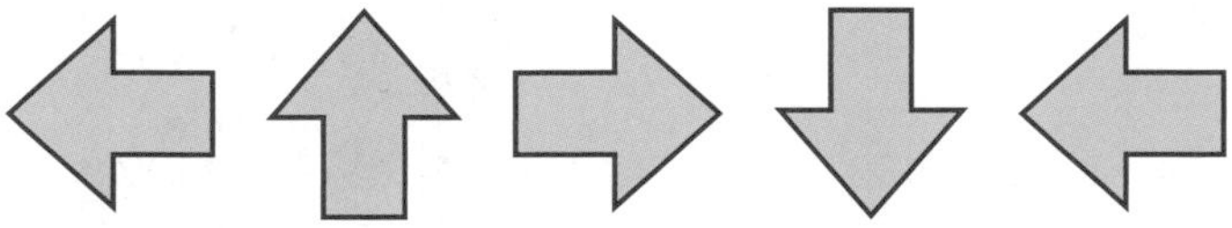

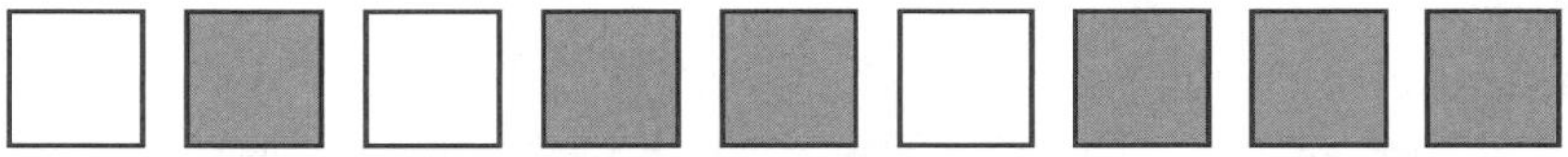

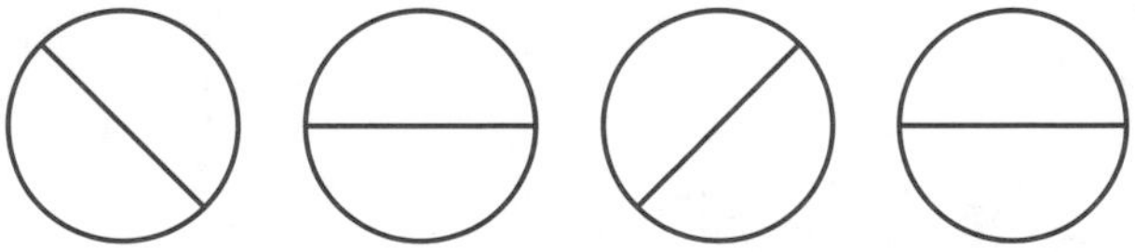

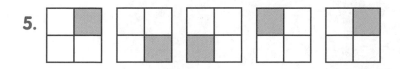

Measure Them

Use an inch ruler to measure the length
of each animal. Write the measurements
to the nearest $\frac{1}{4}$ inch.

_____ in.

_____ in.

_____ in.

_____ in.

_____ in.

Skill Sharpeners: Math • EMC 8254 • © Evan-Moor Corp.

Six students brought their pets to school to show their class.
Use the clues to determine in what order the pets were shown.

Clues

- The mouse was shown before the bird.
- The cat was shown after the bird.
- The dog was shown after the rabbit.
- The fish was shown before the mouse.
- The fish was shown after the dog.

Write the names of the animals in the order they were shown
to the class.

first _____   fourth _____

second _____   fifth _____

third _____   sixth _____

Pet Pals

Rascal's Doghouse

Skill:
Identify lines, line segments, and rays

You can use points and symbols to name a line, line segment, or ray.

Name a **line** using two points on the line.	A B	AB or BA
Name a **line segment** using its endpoints.	A B	$\overline{AB}$ or $\overline{BA}$
Name a **ray** starting with its endpoint and using another point on the ray.	A B $\overrightarrow{AB}$	A B $\overrightarrow{BA}$

Here is Rascal in his doghouse.
Use the picture to name the figures below.

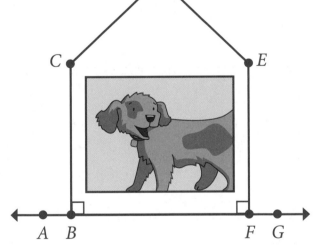

1. Name a line. _____

2. Name a ray that goes toward

   the left. _____

3. Name a ray that goes toward

   the right. _____

4. Name a pair of line segments on the doghouse that are parallel.

   _____, _____

5. Name a pair of line segments on the doghouse that are perpendicular.

   _____, _____

Three Kinds of Angles

An angle is formed by two rays that meet at an endpoint.

A **right angle** is an angle that forms a square corner.

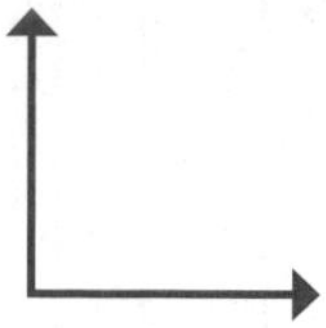

An **acute angle** is smaller than a right angle.

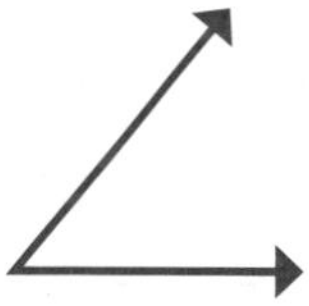

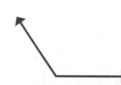

An **obtuse angle** is larger than a right angle.

Identify each of the angles as **right**, **acute**, or **obtuse**.

1. _____

2. _____

3. _____

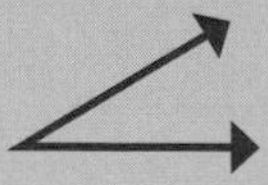

4. _____

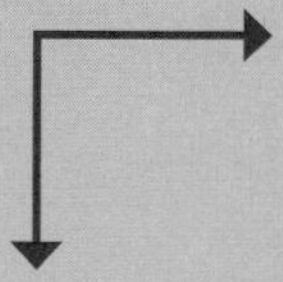

5. _____

6. _____

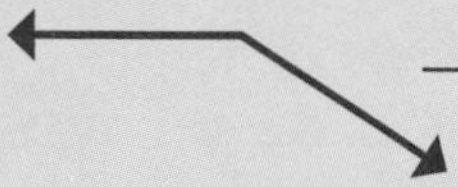

7. _____

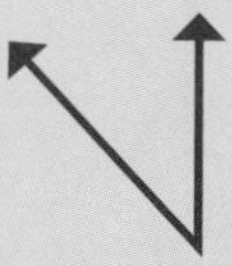

8. _____

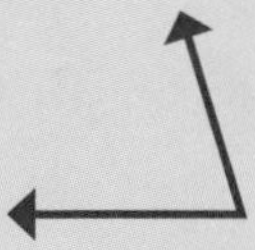

Pet Pals

Write the decimals. Then write **>**, **<**, or **=** in the circles to compare.

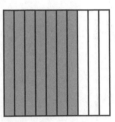  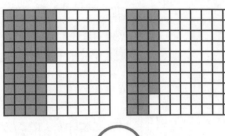

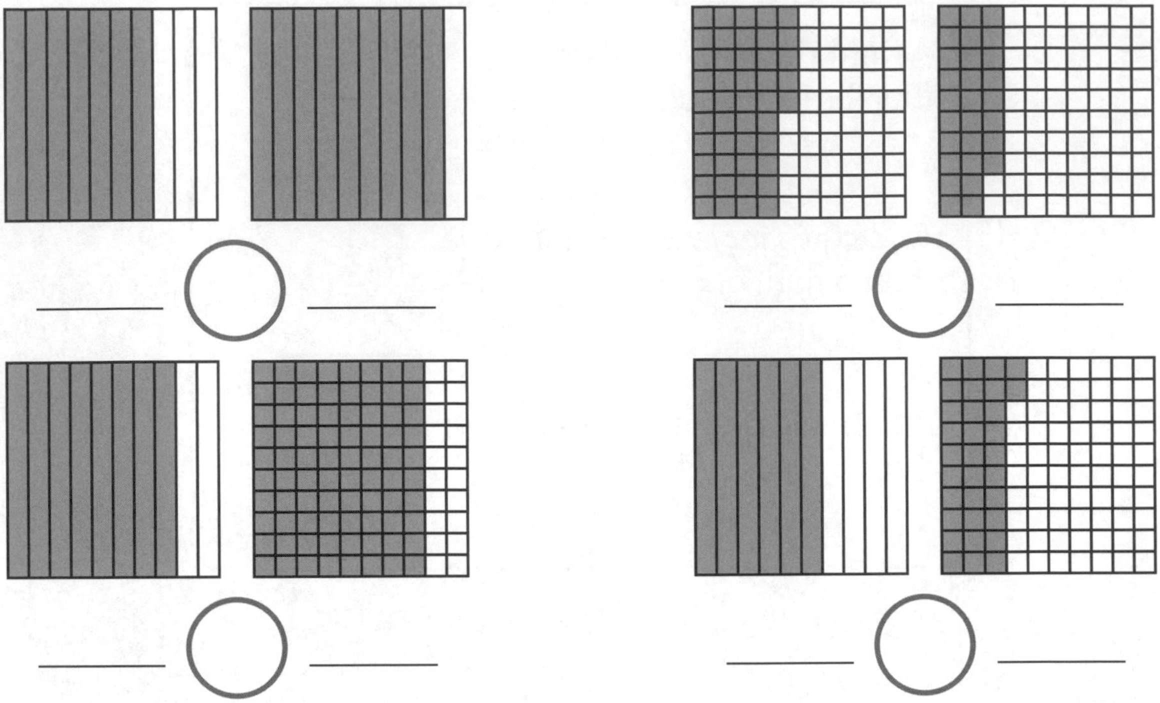

_____ ◯ _____   _____ ◯ _____

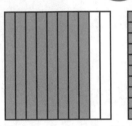 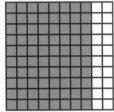 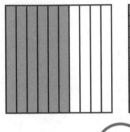 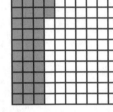

_____ ◯ _____   _____ ◯ _____

Add or subtract.

0.4	1.24	6.1
+ 0.3	+ 0.45	+ 0.77

7.9	9.53	8.7
− 1.2	− 0.43	− 3.69

Round **209,792** to the nearest thousand.

_____

Now round **209,792** to the nearest hundred thousand.

_____

Write the names of the figures using letters and symbols.

a ray _____

a pair of perpendicular line segments

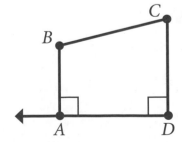

_____, _____

Skill Sharpeners: Math • EMC 8254 • © Evan-Moor Corp.

The books on the shelf are all mixed up! The numbers need to be arranged in order from the smallest to the largest. Write them in order on the lines.

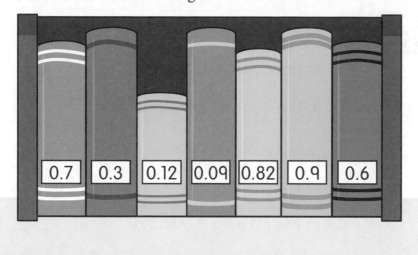

0.7 0.3 0.12 0.09 0.82 0.9 0.6

_____ , _____ , _____ , _____ , _____ , _____ , _____

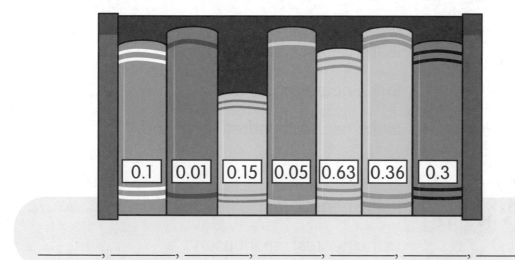

0.1 0.01 0.15 0.05 0.63 0.36 0.3

_____ , _____ , _____ , _____ , _____ , _____ , _____

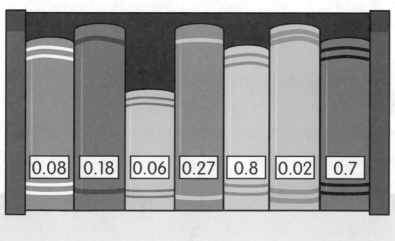

0.08 0.18 0.06 0.27 0.8 0.02 0.7

_____ , _____ , _____ , _____ , _____ , _____ , _____

At the Library

Rounding Time

Round each of the numbers on the books to the place values listed.

1. 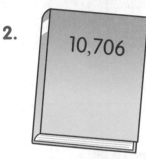 94,830

to the nearest hundred _____

to the nearest thousand _____

to the nearest ten thousand _____

2. 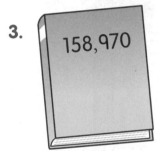 10,706

to the nearest ten _____

to the nearest thousand _____

to the nearest ten thousand _____

3. 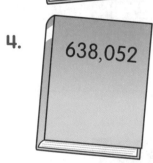 158,970

to the nearest hundred _____

to the nearest thousand _____

to the nearest hundred thousand _____

4. 638,052

to the nearest ten _____

to the nearest ten thousand _____

to the nearest hundred thousand _____

5. Use all six digits below to make a number that
   - is odd,
   - becomes 500,000 when rounded to the nearest ten thousand, and
   - becomes 500,000 when rounded to the nearest hundred thousand.

_____

6   0   9

3   4   2

Hector is looking for a book about scuba diving.
Solve each problem as you find the way through the maze.
Color the path through the maze to help Hector find his book.

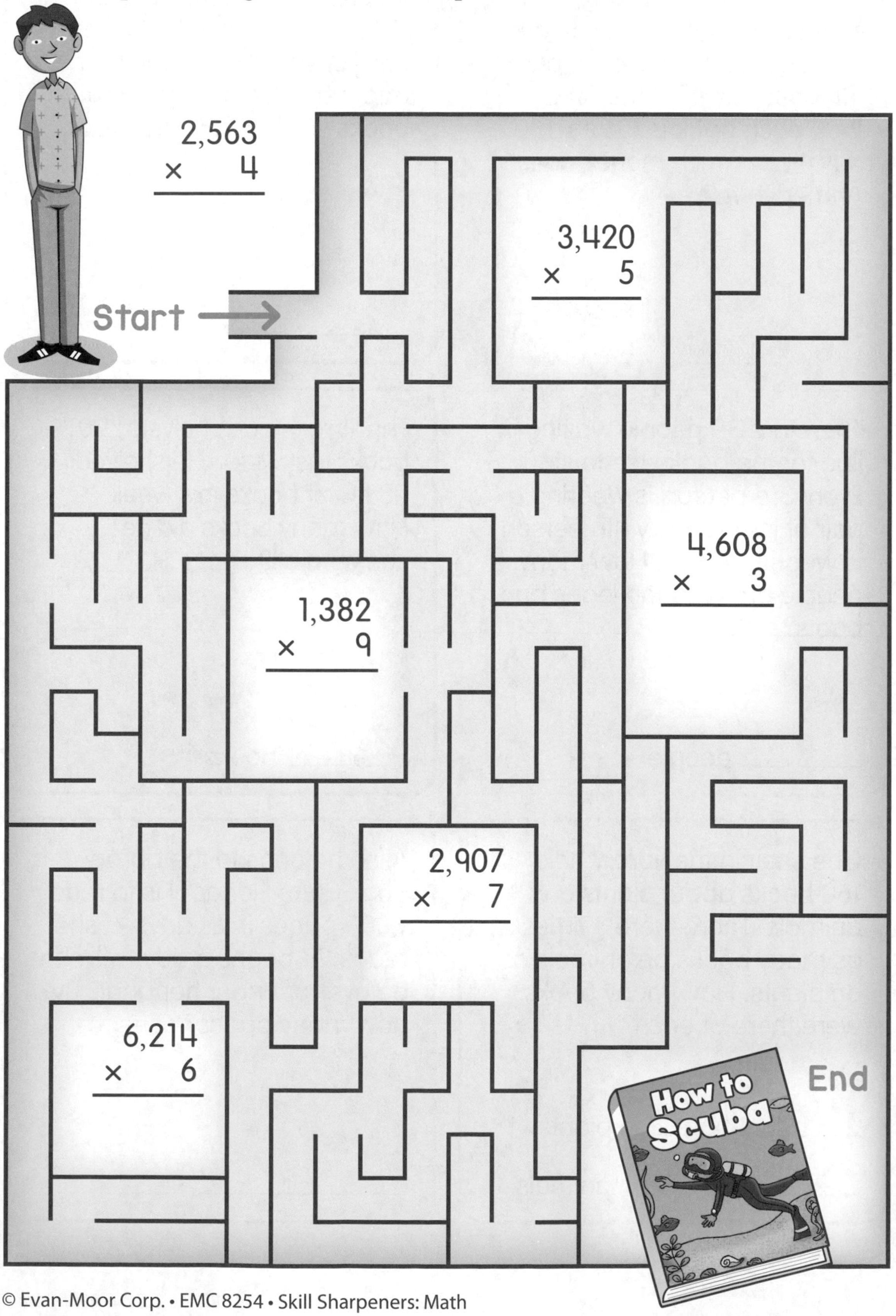

Skill:
Multiply a multidigit number by a 1-digit number

2,563
×   4

Start →

3,420
×   5

4,608
×   3

1,382
×   9

2,907
×   7

6,214
×   6

How to Scuba

End

At the Library

Skill:
Solve word problems

Solve the problems.

Ahmed's library book is 9 days overdue. For the first five days, the fees are 15¢ for each book for each day it is late. After that, each book is 10¢ each day. How much money does Ahmed owe?

$_____

A librarian wants to display 156 new books on 4 shelves. Each shelf will have the same number of books. How many books will be on each shelf?

_____ books

There are 39 people waiting in line for the book sale to start. Every 3rd person is wearing a pair of jeans. Every 4th person is wearing boots. How many people are wearing jeans **and** boots?

_____ people

The library aide shelved 1,401 books last week. He shelved 98 fewer books this week. How many books did he shelve in all?

_____ books

One shelf in the library held 160 books about plants and animals. There were 3 times as many books on animals as on plants. How many books were there of each?

_____ books on plants

_____ books on animals

Alisa belongs to the Library Book Club. Her goal is to read 1,000 pages in 31 days. If she reads 27 pages a day, will she be over or under her goal? By how many pages?

_____

Skill Sharpeners: Math • EMC 8254 • © Evan-Moor Corp.

At the Library

Read the clues to figure out the mystery numbers.

Skills:
Use logical thinking; Find factors and multiples

The number is a factor of 24. It is less than 12. It is a multiple of 2 and 4.

What is the number?

_____

The number is a factor of 40. It is greater than 10. It is a multiple of 5.

What is the number?

_____

The number is a factor of 30. It is greater than 4. It is a multiple of 2 but **not** a multiple of 5.

What is the number?

_____

The number is a factor of 36. It is greater than 6. It is a multiple of 3 but **not** a multiple of 2.

What is the number?

_____

At the Library

Skills:
Add and subtract
mixed numbers

Solve the problems below and write your answers on the lines.
Then match each answer with its letter from the key. Write the
letters in order of the problems to find out on what day Lily checked
out some library books. (You will not use all the letters in the key.)

Key

$1\frac{1}{2}$	**E**	$4\frac{1}{8}$	**R**	$5\frac{3}{4}$	**L**
2	**A**	$4\frac{5}{8}$	**U**	6	**Y**
$3\frac{3}{8}$	**T**	5	**T**	$6\frac{1}{3}$	**S**
$4\frac{1}{10}$	**D**	$5\frac{2}{5}$	**A**	$8\frac{3}{4}$	**S**

1. $3\frac{1}{4} + 2\frac{2}{4} =$ _____

2. $4\frac{1}{2} - 2\frac{1}{2} =$ _____

3. $8\frac{2}{3} - 2\frac{1}{3} =$ _____

4. $9\frac{7}{8} - 6\frac{4}{8} =$ _____

5. $7\frac{4}{5} - 2\frac{4}{5} =$ _____

6. $1\frac{3}{8} + 3\frac{2}{8} =$ _____

7. $5\frac{1}{2} - 4 =$ _____

8. $6\frac{3}{4} + 2 =$ _____

9. $7\frac{3}{10} - 3\frac{2}{10} =$ _____

10. $2\frac{1}{5} + 3\frac{1}{5} =$ _____

11. $3\frac{9}{10} + 2\frac{1}{10} =$ _____

___ ___ ___ ___ ___

___ ___ ___ ___ ___ ___

Skill Sharpeners: Math • EMC 8254 • © Evan-Moor Corp.

At the Library

Write the time below each clock. Then write the matching letters at the bottom of the page to spell out a tongue twister. Say it quickly three times!

Skill:
Tell time to the nearest minute

O

____:____

L

____:____

T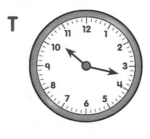

____:____

F

____:____

O

____:____

K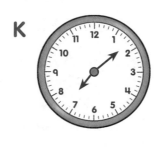

____:____

B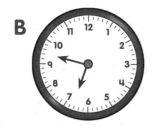

____:____

S

____:____

L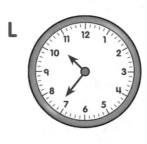

____:____

_____ _____ _____   _____ _____ _____ _____
6:47   2:22   6:47   10:36 8:07 12:43 10:17

_____ _____ _____ _____   _____ _____
5:21   8:07 10:17 12:43   2:22   4:48

_____ _____ _____ _____ _____
6:47   2:22   8:07   7:08 12:43

Solve the problems.

1. Kenichi rode his bike to the library. It took him 16 minutes to get there. He arrived at the library at 11:05.

   At what time did Kenichi leave his home? _____

2. Carla was studying at the library. Suddenly she looked at the clock and said, "Oh no! I've been here for $1\frac{1}{2}$ hours. I have 10 minutes to get home by 5:20 for dinner!"

   At what time did Carla start studying? _____

3. Story Time was held at the library on Saturday morning at 11:15. The librarian spent 25 minutes reading a book aloud to the children. Then they had a snack break for 7 minutes. The librarian finished the book in 14 minutes, and the children had 9 minutes to talk about it.

   At what time did Story Time end? _____

4. The Library Book Club meets at 4:20. The meeting lasts $1\frac{1}{4}$ hours. The club is meeting right now. It is 5:12.

   How much longer is it before the meeting ends? _____

5. Marcus tutored three students at the library yesterday afternoon. He spent 35 minutes with each one. Marcus started tutoring at 1:27. He tutored one student after the other.

   At what time did he finish tutoring?

   _____

Skill Sharpeners: Math • EMC 8254 • © Evan-Moor Corp.

Skill:
Read a line graph

Use the line graph to answer the questions below.

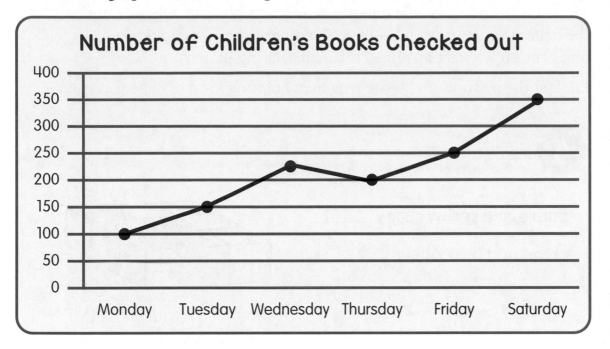

Number of Children's Books Checked Out

1. How many more books were checked out on Tuesday than on Monday? _____ more books

2. About how many books were checked out on Wednesday? _____ books

3. About how many books were checked out in all this week? _____ books

4. On which day was the greatest number of books checked out? _____

5. On which days were at least 200 books checked out?

_____

6. What might be one reason more books were checked out on Saturday than on Monday?

_____

_____

At the Library

How Many Blocks?

A library had large plastic seats that children could sit on during Story Time. Each seat was made out of two different types of cubes. Some of the cubes were purple and yellow. The other cubes were green and blue. The cubes were arranged in an alternating pattern.

Look at the pictures and write how many of each kind of cube was used.

A

purple and yellow cubes _____

green and blue cubes _____

B

purple and yellow cubes _____

green and blue cubes _____

C

purple and yellow cubes _____

green and blue cubes _____

At the Library

Skill Sharpeners: Math • EMC 8254 • © Evan-Moor Corp.

Skill:
Compare
U.S. customary
measures of
length

Jake and Mia are at the entrance of the library. To find out where Jake is going, **circle** the **larger** measure at each question mark. Follow the path with the larger measures until you can go no further. To find out where Mia is going, **underline** the **smaller** measure. Follow the path with the smaller measures until you can go no further. Use the information in the box to help you.

| 1 foot = 12 inches |
| 1 yard = 3 feet |
| 1 mile = 1,760 yards |

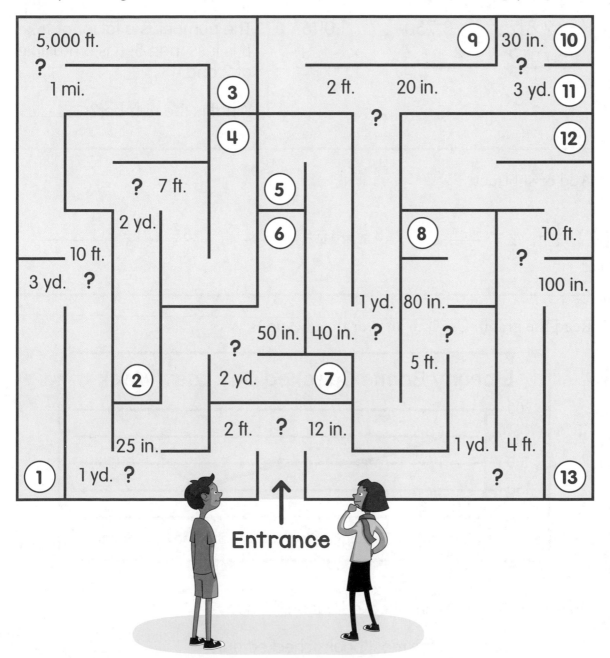

What number was at the end of Jake's path? _____

What number was at the end of Mia's path? _____

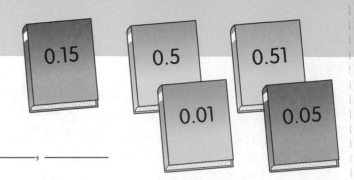

Write the decimals in order from the smallest to the largest.

————, ————, ————, ————, ————

Multiply.

$$2{,}817 \times 5$$

$$8{,}750 \times 2$$

$$1{,}046 \times 9$$

Solve.

The number is a factor of 16. It is less than 5. It is a multiple of 2 and 4.

What is the number? ———

Add or subtract.

$7\frac{1}{2} + 3\frac{1}{2} =$ ———

$8\frac{3}{4} - 3\frac{2}{4} =$ ———

$5\frac{2}{5} + 4\frac{1}{5} =$ ———

Read the graph. Use it to answer the questions.

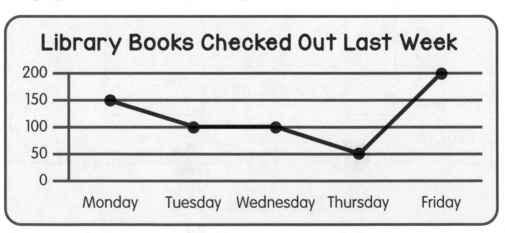

Library Books Checked Out Last Week

How many books were checked out on Tuesday? ———

On which day were the most books checked out? ————

How many books were checked out in all last week? ———

At the Library

Skill Sharpeners: Math • EMC 8254 • © Evan-Moor Corp.

Follow the Path

Skill:
Add, subtract, multiply, and divide within 1,000

Start at the park's entrance. The first problem is **80 × 6**. The answer goes in the next space. Then subtract **20**. Write that answer in the next empty space, and continue this pattern around the path. After completing the path, fill in the blanks below.

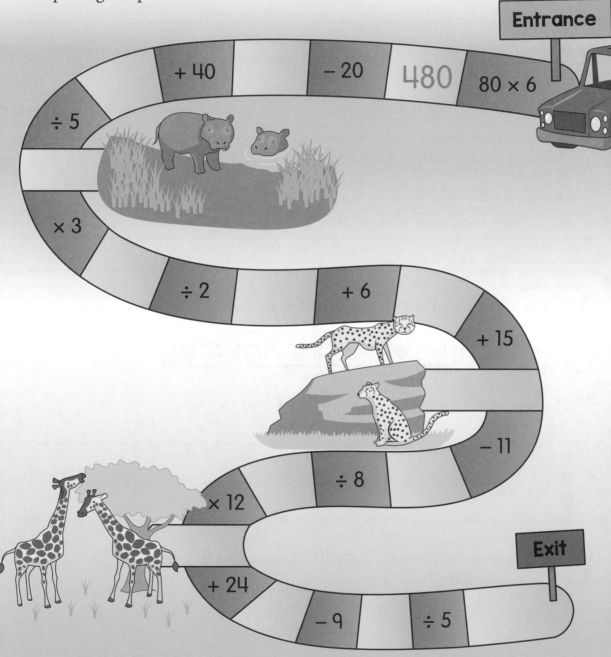

Entrance

+ 40   − 20   480   80 × 6

÷ 5

× 3

÷ 2   + 6   + 15

− 11

÷ 8

× 12

Exit

+ 24   − 9   ÷ 5

Wildlife Park

Write the answer that leads to each location in the wildlife park.

1. Hippos: _____

2. Cheetahs: _____

3. Giraffes: _____

4. Exit: _____

Factors and Multiples

Write all the factors for each of the following numbers.

> **Example: 20—1, 2, 4, 5, 10, 20**

16 _____

12 _____

24 _____

What are the common, or shared, factors of 12, 16, and 24?	Which common factor of 12, 16, and 24 is the greatest number?
_____	_____

Write the first six multiples for each of the following numbers.

> **Example: 5—5, 10, 15, 20, 25, 30**

3 _____

4 _____

6 _____

What is the least common multiple (the lowest multiple that 3, 4, and 6 share)?

_____

Skill Sharpeners: Math • EMC 8254 • © Evan-Moor Corp.

Wildlife Park

Division Puzzlers

Read the clues. Use division to help you find the mystery numbers.

Skills:
Use logical thinking; Divide with remainders

I am greater than 20 but less than 30.

Divide me by 2, and you get a remainder of 1.

Divide me by 3, and you get a remainder of 2.

Divide me by 4, and you get a remainder of 3.

What number am I? _____

I am greater than 30 but less than 40.

Divide me by 2, and you get a remainder of 0.

Divide me by 3, and you get a remainder of 1.

Divide me by 4, and you get a remainder of 2.

What number am I? _____

I am greater than 40 but less than 50.

Divide me by 2, and you get a remainder of 1.

Divide me by 4, and you get a remainder of 3.

Divide me by 6, and you get a remainder of 5.

What number am I? _____

I am greater than 60 but less than 70.

Divide me by 3, and you get a remainder of 2.

Divide me by 4, and you get a remainder of 2.

Divide me by 5, and you get a remainder of 2.

What number am I? _____

Wildlife Park

Moms and Babies

Solve the problems.

Flappy, a baby elephant, weighed 200 pounds at birth. Her mother was 30 times heavier!

How much did Flappy's mother weigh?

_____ pounds

Nala, a newborn tiger cub, weighed 3 pounds. His mother was 240 pounds.

How many times heavier was the mother than her cub?

_____ times heavier

A five-month-old hippo weighed 300 pounds. That was only $\frac{1}{10}$ the weight of her mother.

How much did the mother hippo weigh?

_____ pounds

A one-year-old lion cub weighed 50 pounds. His mother weighed 6 times more.

How much did the lion cub's mother weigh?

_____ pounds

Patch, a baby giraffe, weighed 150 pounds. His mother was 16 times heavier.

How much did Patch's mother weigh?

_____ pounds

A mother zebra weighed 750 pounds. Her baby was only $\frac{1}{10}$ her weight.

How much did the baby zebra weigh?

_____ pounds

Skill Sharpeners: Math • EMC 8254 • © Evan-Moor Corp.

A Place to Play

Skills:
Determine area
and perimeter;
Explain thinking

A new play area is being built for the monkeys. Find its perimeter and area.

6 ft.

5 ft.

5 ft.

10 ft.

9 ft.

13 ft.

8 ft.

20 ft.

perimeter: _____ feet   **area:** _____ square feet

Explain how you solved the problem.

_____

_____

_____

_____

Wildlife Park

Let's Eat!

Skills:

Extend patterns;
Multiply a
multidigit
number by a
1-digit number

Complete each table. Then complete the sentences at the bottom of the page.

1. A giant panda eats 25 pounds of food a day.

day	1	2	3	4	5
food (pounds)	25				

2. An elephant eats 300 pounds of food a day.

day	1	2	3	4	5
food (pounds)					

3. A giraffe eats 75 pounds of food a day.

day	1	2	3	4	5
food (pounds)					

4. A deer eats 2.5 pounds of food a day.

day	1	2	3	4	5
food (pounds)					

5. By day 10, a giraffe will have eaten a total of _____ pounds.

6. A giant panda will have eaten a total of 500 pounds

   on day _____.

7. After 8 days, an elephant will have eaten _____ more pounds than a deer.

Wildlife Park

Skill:
Create patterns

Create patterns to show possible solutions to the problems.

1. Selina is making a banner for Wildlife Park, where she works. She would like to create a pattern of triangles for a border along the bottom of the banner. The triangles can be different sizes and they can be pointing different ways. Draw a pattern she could use.

Welcome to Wildlife Park!

2. Aaron is making a brick fence around the park. He will be using bricks that are shaped like squares and rectangles. Aaron would like to use twice as many squares as rectangles. Draw a pattern he could use.

3. Chandra is going to decorate the arched entrance to the African Plains area. She will use yellow and brown paint, and she wants to create an interesting pattern. Draw a pattern she could use.

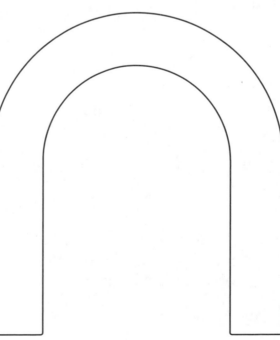

Wildlife Park

We're Thirsty!

Write the equivalent measures. Use the information in the box to help you.

> **Customary Units of Capacity**
>
> 8 ounces = 1 cup
> 2 cups   = 1 pint
> 2 pints = 1 quart
> 4 quarts = 1 gallon

1. How many cups would be needed to fill each container?

   1 quart = _____ cups   1 gallon = _____ cups

   3 quarts = _____ cups   2 pints = _____ cups

2. How many pints would be needed to fill each container?

   1 quart = _____ pints   1 gallon = _____ pints

   5 quarts = _____ pints $2\frac{1}{2}$ gallons = _____ pints

---

Write **>**, **<**, or **=** to compare the amounts.

3. 2 cups ◯ 1 quart   16 ounces ◯ 1 pint

4. 2 pints ◯ 3 cups   9 cups ◯ 2 quarts

5. 2 quarts ◯ 64 ounces   6 pints ◯ 1 gallon

---

6. A person drinks about 8 cups of water a day. An elephant drinks 100 times that amount! How many cups and how many gallons is that?

   _____ cups   _____ gallons

Wildlife Park

Who's Who?

Figure out the names of the animals below. Read the clues to help you fill in the table. When you know that an animal and a name do **not** go together, make an **X** under that name and across from that animal. When you know that an animal and a name **do** go together, write **YES** in that box.

Clues

- Comet is not a bear or a giraffe.
- Stretch is not a giraffe or a zebra.
- Happy is a bear or a lion.
- Rocky is a lion or a crocodile.
- Happy likes to eat fish.
- Rocky does not have hair or fur.

	Comet	Happy	Rocky	Gobi	Stretch
bear					
giraffe					
lion					
crocodile					
zebra					

Write the names beside the correct animals.

bear _____

giraffe _____

lion _____

crocodile _____

zebra _____

Wildlife Park

Angles and Circles

You can use circles to help you find the measures of angles. Angles are measured in degrees. A whole circle measures 360° (360 degrees).

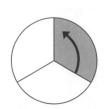

This circle is divided into three equal parts. One angle is one-third of 360 degrees.

The angle measure is 120° because $\frac{1}{3}$ of 360° is 120°.

Write the measure of each angle. Explain how you know.

1. 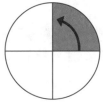 Angle measure

_____°

How do you know?

_____

_____

_____

2. 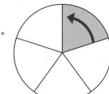 Angle measure

_____°

How do you know?

_____

_____

_____

3.  Angle measure

_____°

How do you know?

_____

_____

_____

4. 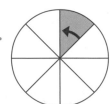 Angle measure

_____°

How do you know?

_____

_____

_____

Wildlife Park

You can use a protractor to measure angles. Line up one side of the angle along the bottom of the protractor. Then, starting at 0°, follow the numbers until you see where the other side of the angle touches the protractor.

This angle measure is 110°.

Write the measure of each angle.

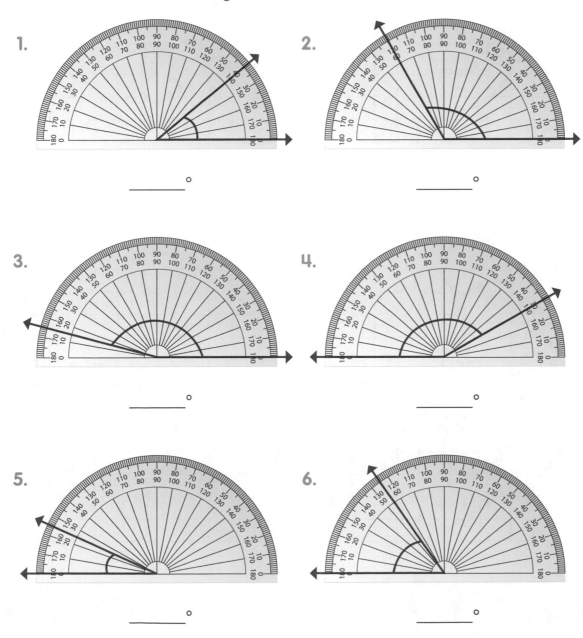

1. _____ °

2. _____ °

3. _____ °

4. _____ °

5. _____ °

6. _____ °

Wildlife Park

Animal Symmetry

Draw the missing half of each animal's face, and write the name of the animal below its picture. Then in the blank grid, draw your own picture of a symmetrical face. The face may be of a person or another animal.

_____

_____

_____

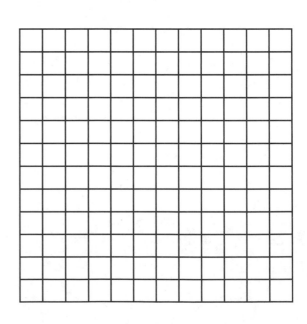

_____

Write all the common factors of each set of numbers.

12, 18, 24 _____

15, 30, 45 _____

Write the least common multiple for each set of numbers.

2, 3, 5 _____

6, 8, 12 _____

Complete the table. Then answer the question.

A giraffe eats 75 pounds of food a day.
On what day will it have eaten a total of 600 pounds?   day _____

day	1	2	3	4	5
food (pounds)					

Use the information in the box to help you write equivalent amounts.

2 pints = _____ cups

3 quarts = _____ pints

4 gallons = _____ quarts

1 gallon = _____ ounces

8 ounces = 1 cup
2 cups   = 1 pint
2 pints   = 1 quart
4 quarts = 1 gallon

Write the measure of each angle.

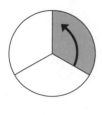

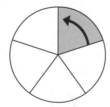

_____ °   _____ °   _____ °

Wildlife Park

A Bicycle Riddle

Skill:
Add within
100,000

Why can't bicycles stand by themselves?

To solve the riddle, first write the sums for the problems below.
Then write the matching letters on the lines at the bottom of the page.

T $1,407 + 21,209 =$ _____

E $9,519 + 45 =$ _____

E $913 + 289 =$ _____

R $45 + 132 + 5,084 =$ _____

I $256 + 250 + 831 =$ _____

O $290 + 491 + 502 =$ _____

Y $805 + 75 + 9,490 =$ _____

D $1,899 + 307 + 804 =$ _____

T $6,503 + 7,303 =$ _____

T $802 + 407 + 842 =$ _____

E $735 + 285 + 482 =$ _____

A $375 + 493 + 263 =$ _____

R $907 + 32 + 284 =$ _____

W $280 + 481 + 427 =$ _____

H $285 + 429 + 492 =$ _____

Because _____ _____ _____ _____
22,616   1,206   9,564   10,370

_____ _____ _____   _____ _____ _____
1,131   5,261   1,202   13,806   1,188   1,283

_____ _____ _____ _____ _____
2,051   1,337   1,223   1,502   3,010

Sports World

Skill Sharpeners: Math • EMC 8254 • © Evan-Moor Corp.

Jayden needs to get from the park entrance to the stadium. In order to walk along any path, he must give the gatekeeper the number of tickets that are noted on the path. Jayden has 98 tickets. He must use all of them to enter the stadium. Which paths can he follow to the stadium? Trace over the paths to show your answer.

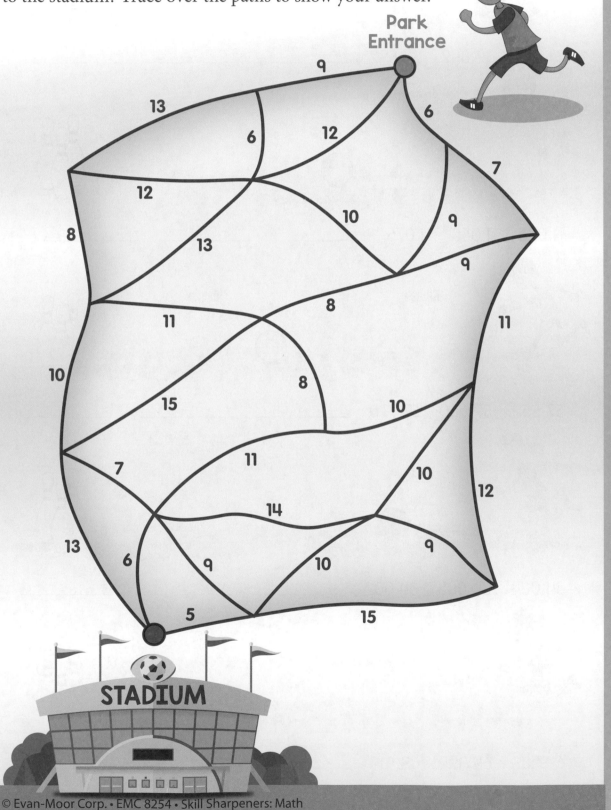

Sports World

Knock 'Em Down!

Write the next three numbers in each pattern
to knock down the pins in each bowling lane.

31,892   32,892   33,892   _____ _____ _____

 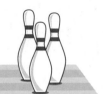

11,025   11,050   11,075   _____ _____ _____

 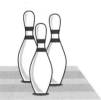

57,550   57,660   57,770   _____ _____ _____

84,004   84,003   84,002   _____ _____ _____

69,939   69,929   69,919   _____ _____ _____

Sports World

Solve the problems.

Brianna goes to soccer practice every day. Each time, she practices for one hour. So far today, she has practiced for $\frac{1}{3}$ hour.

What fraction of an hour is left until her practice is over?

_____ hour

How many minutes is that?

_____ minutes

Yumi practices swimming at the local community pool. The pool is twice as long as it is wide.

The perimeter of the pool is 150 feet. What is the pool's length? What is its width?

length _____ feet

width _____ feet

Ian practices basketball with his friend. He usually shoots 8 baskets at every practice.

How many baskets would he shoot after 15 practices?

_____ baskets

How many practices would it take for him to shoot 200 baskets?

_____ practices

Raj practices tennis three times a week. Each time he practices for $1\frac{1}{2}$ hours.

How many hours does Raj practice tennis in one week?

_____ hours

Suppose Raj practiced for a total of 18 hours. How many practices was that?

_____ practices

Sports World

At the Track Meet

Some runners are ready to compete at the track meet.
The Venn diagram shows the number of runners for two races.

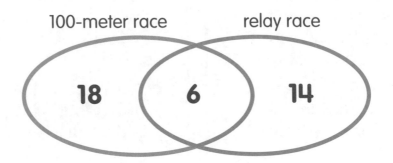

1. How many runners will compete in **only**
   the 100-meter race?   _____ runners

2. How many runners will compete in **only**
   the relay race?   _____ runners

3. How many runners in all will compete
   in the 100-meter race?   _____ runners

4. How many runners in all will compete
   in the relay race?   _____ runners

5. How many runners will compete in at least one race? _____ runners

6. Suppose a runner who was planning to run in both races
   drops out because of illness. What would the Venn diagram
   look like then? Write your answer below.

How do baseball players stay cool?

To find the answer to the riddle, look at the sets of numbers below. Each set is a list of factors. First, write the least common multiple for each set. Then write the matching letters on the lines at the bottom of the page.

A 3, 4, 6   _12_   O 3, 6, 8   _____

E 1, 2, 3   _____   S 3, 7, 14 _____

F 1, 2, 7   _____   T 2, 6, 9   _____

H 5, 9, 15 _____   X 2, 4, 7   _____

I 8, 10, 20 _____   Y 3, 4, 9   _____

N 3, 5, 10 _____

___ ___ ___ ___   ___ ___ ___
18   45   6   36   42   40   18

___ ___ ___ ___   ___ ___
30   6   28   18   18   24

___ ___ ___   ___ ___ ___ ___
18   45   6   14   12   30   42

What's Your Estimate?

Skills:
Make estimates;
Explain thinking

Give an estimate for each answer below. Do **not** compute the exact answer. Then use numbers or words to explain how you made your estimate.

What is a good estimate for 11 × 35?

_____
estimate

Explain.

What is a good estimate for the sum of 299 and 503?

_____
estimate

Explain.

What is a good estimate for 604 – 98?

_____
estimate

Explain.

What is a good estimate for the product of 8,013 and 2?

_____
estimate

Explain.

What is a good estimate for how many times 9 goes into 2,675?

_____
estimate

Explain.

What is a good estimate for 1,971 + 4,156?

_____
estimate

Explain.

Skill Sharpeners: Math • EMC 8254 • © Evan-Moor Corp.

Skill:
Add and subtract decimals

Solve the problems. Then write the answers in order from smallest to largest on the lines below. Write the corresponding letter for each answer in the boxes to find out what sport Mei plays.

E 0.04
+ 0.05

A 0.27
+ 1.19

P 3.2
− 2.3

G 5.65
− 2.6

M 7.15
− 7.1

F 1.04
+ 3.48

O 9.1
− 5.5

L 0.08
+ 1.12

S 3.59
− 0.7

I 1.09
− 0.99

L 2.18
+ 2.07

Y 0.45
+ 1.63

Skill:
Use logical thinking

Use the clues below to figure out the color and number of each shape on the field. All the numbers are less than **10**. Color each figure and write its number in the shape.

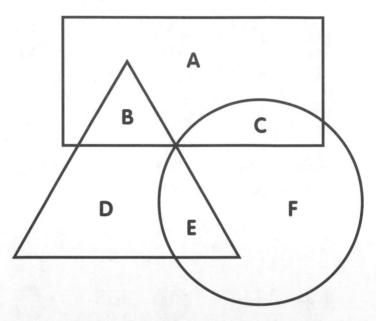

- The sum for the triangle is 15.
- The section that is in the circle and the rectangle is brown.
- The rectangle has orange, yellow, and brown sections.
- The orange section is the number 4.
- The product of the B section and the blue section is 8.
- The 9 section is green.
- The A section is yellow.
- The sum for the rectangle is 17.
- The E section is green.
- The sum for the circle is 24.
- The sum of the A section and the B section is 9.
- The F section is purple.

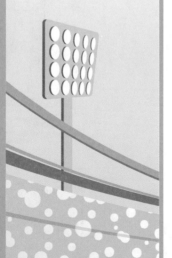

Skill Sharpeners: Math • EMC 8254 • © Evan-Moor Corp.

Skill:
Describe shapes
by types of lines
and angles

Complete the table to describe each shape. Then draw and describe
your own shape at the bottom of the table.

Shape	How many sides?	What type of angles? (acute, right, obtuse) How many?	Are there pairs of parallel sides or perpendicular sides?
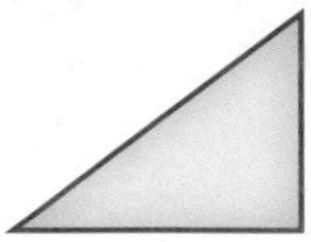	3	1 right angle, 2 acute angles	1 pair of perpendicular sides

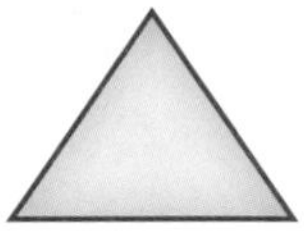			
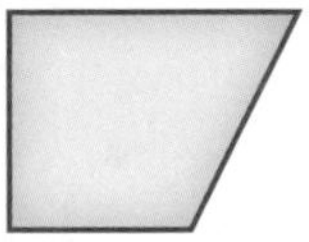			
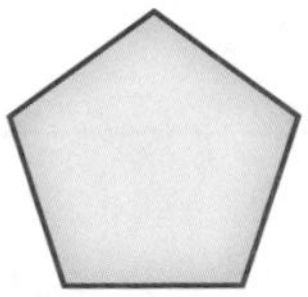			

Sports World

Hooray for Shapes!

Read the pair of descriptions in each row. Write the number of each shape under each description that describes it. At the bottom, write another pair of descriptions and group the shapes.

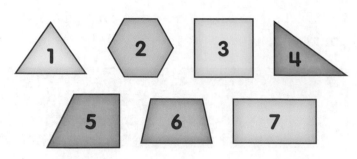

1. Has perpendicular lines	Has no perpendicular lines
2. Has parallel lines	Has no parallel lines
3. Has obtuse angles	Has no obtuse angles
4. _____	_____

Add.

```
       83            9,475
    8,964              632
  +   758          + 1,084
  _____          _____
```

Add or subtract.

```
    3.9         7.93         5.1
  + 0.17      - 1.25      - 2.83
  _____      _____      _____
```

Write the next three numbers in each pattern.

25,715   26,715   27,715   _____   _____   _____

83,590   83,490   83,390   _____   _____   _____

Use the Venn diagram to answer the questions.

100-meter race   400-meter race

How many in all competed in the 100-meter race?

12   **4**   **8**

_____

How many competed in **only** the 400-meter race? _____

Circle the shapes that have at least one pair of parallel lines.

Circle the shapes that have at least one pair of perpendicular lines.

Sports World

Let's Go!

Skill:
Multiply a multidigit number by a 1-digit number

Multiply.

$$\begin{array}{r} 7{,}106 \\ \times\quad 3 \\ \hline \end{array}$$

$$\begin{array}{r} 3{,}095 \\ \times\quad 4 \\ \hline \end{array}$$

$$\begin{array}{r} 2{,}740 \\ \times\quad 6 \\ \hline \end{array}$$

$$\begin{array}{r} 2{,}076 \\ \times\quad 5 \\ \hline \end{array}$$

$$\begin{array}{r} 1{,}851 \\ \times\quad 8 \\ \hline \end{array}$$

$$\begin{array}{r} 4{,}190 \\ \times\quad 6 \\ \hline \end{array}$$

$$\begin{array}{r} 7{,}301 \\ \times\quad 9 \\ \hline \end{array}$$

$$\begin{array}{r} 5{,}060 \\ \times\quad 2 \\ \hline \end{array}$$

$$\begin{array}{r} 6{,}420 \\ \times\quad 7 \\ \hline \end{array}$$

Look at your answers.

Which product is the largest? _____

Which product is the smallest? _____

Skill Sharpeners: Math • EMC 8254 • © Evan-Moor Corp.

Skill:
Divide without remainders

What did the car have on its toast this morning?

To solve the riddle, first solve each problem below.
Then write the matching letters on the lines at the bottom of the page.

A

2)714

C

4)980

F

5)925

I

6)2,472

J

8)4,184

M

7)3,591

R

5)1,485

T

9)2,502

278	297	357	185	185	412	245

| | 523 | 357 | 513 |

On the Move

Travel Tales

Solve the problems.

Show Your Work

1. There were 3 cruise ships in the harbor. Each one held 2,789 passengers. How many passengers were there in all?

_____ passengers

2. A bus company had 12 buses. Each bus carried 84 passengers. How many passengers could the bus company carry at one time?

_____ passengers

3. There were 1,040 passengers on a train. The train had 8 cars. If each car had the same number of people, how many people were in each car?

_____ people

4. A plane needed to fly 1,500 miles. It traveled 500 miles per hour. How long was the flight?

_____ hours

5. A helicopter traveled 120 miles an hour for $1\frac{1}{2}$ hours. How far did it travel?

_____ miles

Skills:
Use logical
thinking; Find
factors and
multiples

Read each set of clues. Write the mystery number.

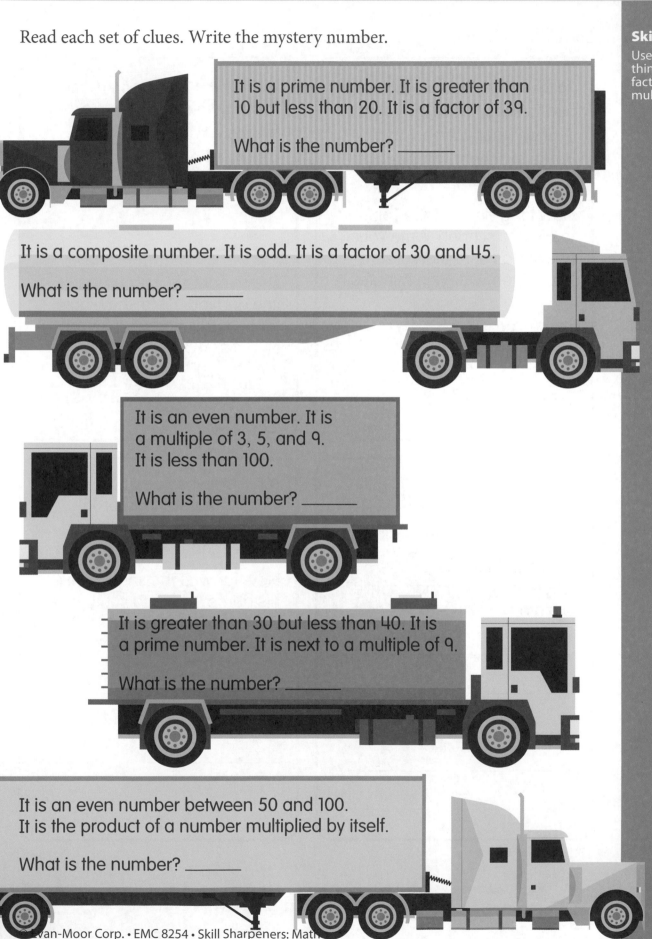

It is a prime number. It is greater than
10 but less than 20. It is a factor of 39.

What is the number? _____

It is a composite number. It is odd. It is a factor of 30 and 45.

What is the number? _____

It is an even number. It is
a multiple of 3, 5, and 9.
It is less than 100.

What is the number? _____

It is greater than 30 but less than 40. It is
a prime number. It is next to a multiple of 9.

What is the number? _____

It is an even number between 50 and 100.
It is the product of a number multiplied by itself.

What is the number? _____

On the Move

Skills:
Solve word problems; Add and subtract fractions; Explain thinking

Solve the problems.

Tobin's mom usually drives him to school. The trip takes $\frac{1}{6}$ of an hour. When Tobin walks to school, it takes him 3 times as long.

How long does it take Tobin to walk to school? Write your answer as a fraction of an hour. Then write it in minutes.

_____ hour

_____ minutes

Nadia biked $\frac{50}{100}$ mile to Jamie's home. Then the two friends biked $\frac{45}{100}$ mile to Lenora's home.

How far did Nadia bike in all?

_____

Draw a dot on the number line and label it to show how far Lenora's home was from Nadia's.

Nadia's home

0 mile ●————|————| 1 mile

Ms. Medrano drove $\frac{70}{100}$ mile to the grocery store. Then she drove $\frac{35}{100}$ mile to the mall.

Was Ms. Medrano's drive longer or shorter than a mile? Explain.

_____

_____

_____

_____

Mr. Hamwi drove at a speed of 40 miles an hour for 15 minutes to get to the lawn mower shop.

How far was the shop from his home? How do you know?

_____

_____

_____

_____

_____

Skill Sharpeners: Math • EMC 8254 • © Evan-Moor Corp.

Fancy Flights Airlines allows passengers to take carry-on luggage weighing up to 22.5 kilograms.

> ### Metric Units of Weight
> 1,000 grams (g) = 1 kilogram (kg)

1. Look at the weights of the luggage. Can each suitcase be taken as carry-on luggage? Write **yes** or **no**.

21,000 g   220,000 g   100,000 g

20,000 g   19,000 g   109,000 g

2. Here are the weights of six suitcases. Arrange them in order from the lightest to the heaviest and write them on the lines.

18.5 kg   19,050 g   19.5 kg   19,000 g   18,000 g   18,050 g

_____,   _____,   _____,

_____,   _____,   _____,

3. Ayssel's suitcase weighs 6.5 kg when it is empty. She wants to carry it on the plane with her when she travels. What is the maximum weight she can add to the suitcase? Write your answer in both kilograms and grams.

_____ kg   _____ g

On the Move

Fancy Flights Airlines serves a variety of refreshing drinks during its flights. The circle graph shows what fraction of the passengers chose which drinks. Use the graph to answer the questions.

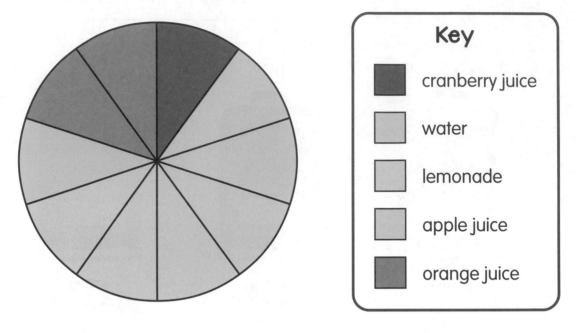

Key

■ cranberry juice

□ water

□ lemonade

□ apple juice

■ orange juice

1. Which drink was chosen the most often? _____

   What fraction of the people chose that drink? _____

2. What fraction of the people chose apple juice? _____

3. Which drink was more popular—cranberry juice or lemonade? _____

4. Suppose there were 200 passengers on the flight. Write how many people chose each drink.

   cranberry juice _____

   water _____

   lemonade _____

   apple juice _____

   orange juice _____

Skill Sharpeners: Math • EMC 8254 • © Evan-Moor Corp.

Draw line segments to complete the picture. Cross out the segments from the list as you draw them. One segment has been done for you.

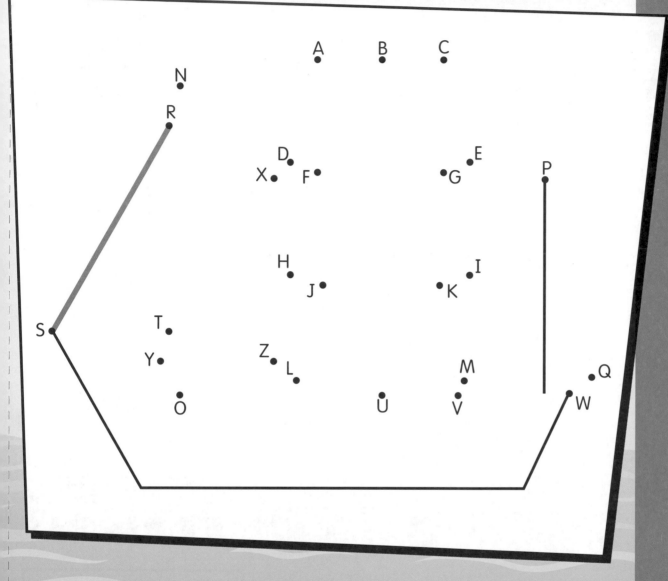

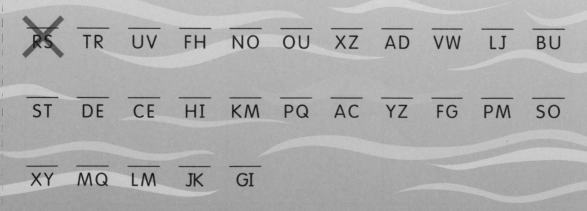

~~RS~~	TR	UV	FH	NO	OU	XZ	AD	VW	LJ	BU
ST	DE	CE	HI	KM	PQ	AC	YZ	FG	PM	SO
XY	MQ	LM	JK	GI						

Search for Angles

Skill:
Classify angles

Look at the angles in each picture. Label them **a**, **o**, or **r**. Then count how many of each angle each picture has.

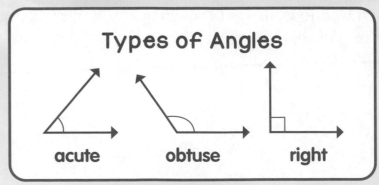

Types of Angles

acute   obtuse   right

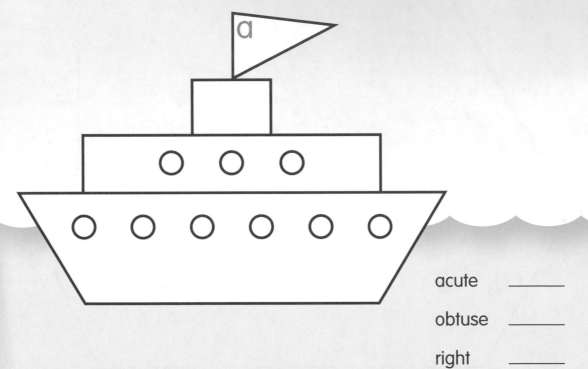

a

acute _____

obtuse _____

right _____

acute _____

obtuse _____

right _____

On the Move

Skills:
Find angle measures;
Explain thinking

Example: You can add the measures of smaller angles to find the measure of a larger angle.

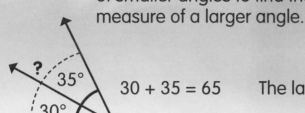

$30 + 35 = 65$ The larger angle is 65°.

Find the unknown angle measure shown by a dotted line.

1.
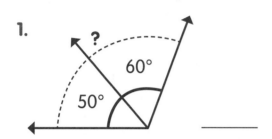

_____

2.
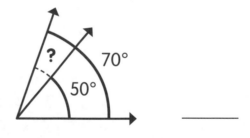

_____

3.
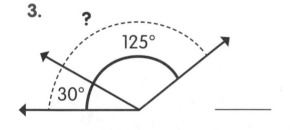

_____

4.

_____

Find the unknown angle measure.

5. A plane circled an airport waiting to land. It moved around 150° and then another 80°. How many more degrees will the plane travel before it returns to its starting position? Explain your answer.

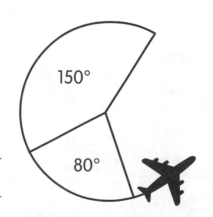

_____

_____

_____

On the Move

Train of Shapes

Draw the shapes in the Venn diagrams to match the descriptions.

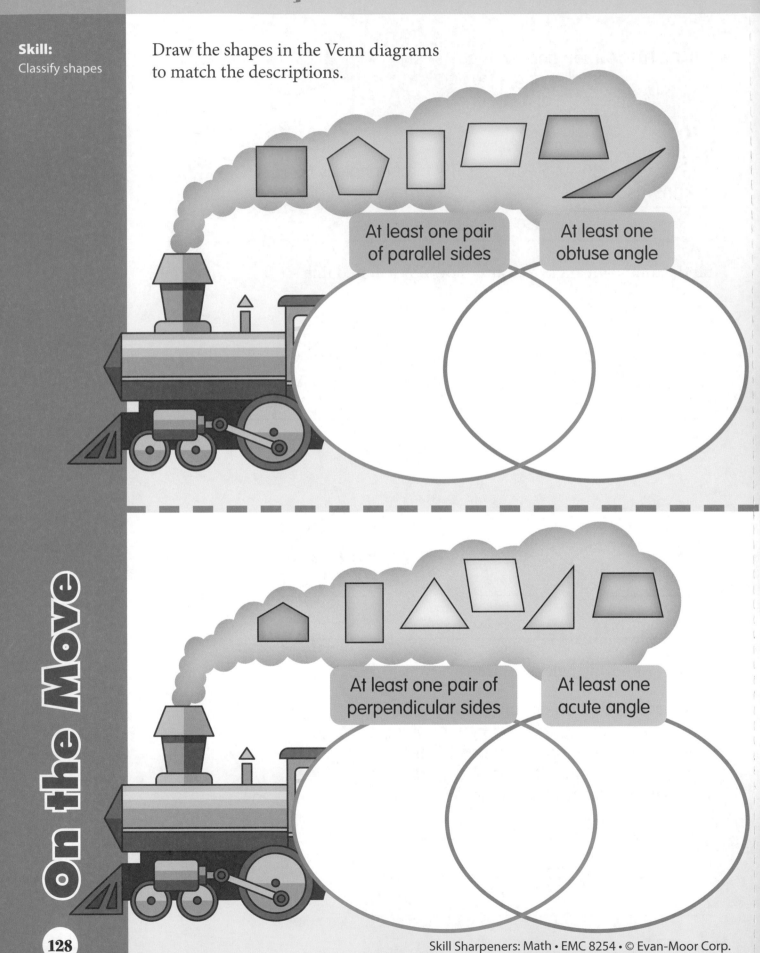

At least one pair of parallel sides

At least one obtuse angle

At least one pair of perpendicular sides

At least one acute angle

On the Move

Skill Sharpeners: Math • EMC 8254 • © Evan-Moor Corp.

You can classify triangles based on their angle measures.

An **acute triangle** has three acute angles.

An **obtuse triangle** has one obtuse angle.

A **right triangle** has one right angle.

Write **acute**, **right**, or **obtuse** to describe each of the boats' sails.

_____   _____   _____

_____   _____   _____

Draw a sailboat that has at least two different triangles for sails. Label the kinds of triangles you used.

On the Move

Multiply.

$$\begin{array}{r} 86 \\ \times\,24 \\ \hline \end{array} \qquad \begin{array}{r} 35 \\ \times\,17 \\ \hline \end{array} \qquad \begin{array}{r} 63 \\ \times\,49 \\ \hline \end{array}$$

Divide.

$$4\overline{)1,424} \qquad 7\overline{)2,163} \qquad 5\overline{)1,085}$$

Solve the problems.

A plane traveled at a speed of 480 miles an hour. How far did it travel in 30 minutes?

_____ miles

A helicopter traveled at 120 miles an hour. How far did it travel in $1\frac{1}{2}$ hours?

_____ miles

Write equivalent measures.

| 1,000 g = 1 kg |

2,000 g = _____ kg

58 kg = _____ g

2.5 kg = _____ g

Write the missing angle measures.

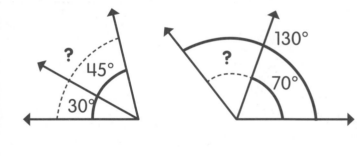

_____   _____

Draw the shapes correctly in the Venn diagram.

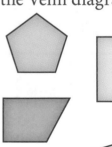

At least one pair of parallel sides   At least one obtuse angle

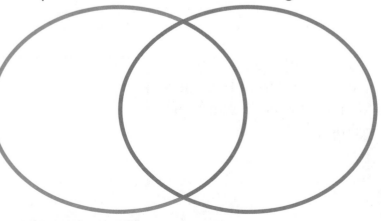

Skill Sharpeners: Math • EMC 8254 • © Evan-Moor Corp.

Answer Key

Page 6

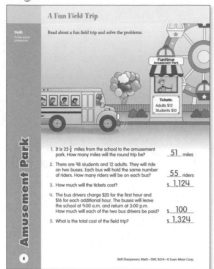

A Fun Field Trip

Read about a fun field trip and solve the problems.

1. It is $25\frac{1}{2}$ miles from the school to the amusement park. How many miles will the round trip be? **51** miles

2. There are 98 students and 12 adults. They will ride on two buses. Each bus will hold the same number of riders. How many riders will be on each bus? **55** riders

3. How much will the tickets cost? $ **1,124**

4. The bus drivers charge $20 for the first hour and $16 for each additional hour. The buses will leave the school at 9:00 a.m. and return at 3:00 p.m. How much will each of the two bus drivers be paid? $ **100**

5. What is the total cost of the field trip? $ **1,324**

Page 7

Let's Go!

Draw a path to help the children reach the rides. Begin at Start. Stop at each circled number. Decide whether it is odd or even and take the path that matches. Continue until you reach the park.

Page 8

Wonderlands

Start at the park's entrance. The first problem reads 8 × 3. The answer goes in the next space. Then subtract 20. Write that answer in the next empty space, and continue this pattern around the path. After completing the path, fill in the blanks below.

Write the answer that leads to each location in the amusement park.

1. Pirates' Paradise: **2**
2. Candy Island: **16**
3. Dinosaurs' World: **30**
4. Exit: **60**

Page 9

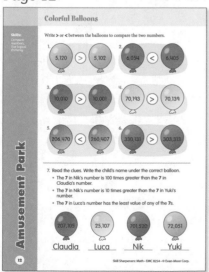

Mystery Ride

Find out which ride Reynaldo went on first. Solve the problems. Then write the matching letters in order on the lines at the bottom of the page.

150 = U	540 = E
240 = J	560 = L
300 = F	600 = E
400 = R	640 = M
420 = G	750 = C
450 = N	800 = D
500 = T	900 = I

1. 6 × 40 = **240**
2. 3 × 50 = **150**
3. 5 × 90 = **450**
4. 60 × 7 = **420**
5. 70 × 8 = **560**
6. 90 × 6 = **540**
7. 2 × 200 = **400**
8. 3 × 300 = **900**
9. 200 × 4 = **800**
10. 200 × 3 = **600**

J U N G L E R I D E

Page 10

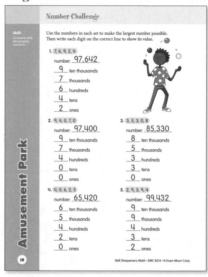

Number Challenge

Use the numbers in each set to make the largest number possible. Then write each digit on the correct line to show its value.

1. 7, 6, 9, 2, 4
number: **97,642**
9 ten thousands
7 thousands
6 hundreds
4 tens
2 ones

2. 9, 4, 0, 7, 0
number: **97,400**
9 ten thousands
7 thousands
4 hundreds
0 tens
0 ones

3. 3, 5, 3, 0, 8
number: **85,330**
8 ten thousands
5 thousands
3 hundreds
3 tens
0 ones

4. 4, 0, 6, 2, 5
number: **65,420**
6 ten thousands
5 thousands
4 hundreds
2 tens
0 ones

5. 2, 9, 3, 4, 4
number: **99,432**
9 ten thousands
9 thousands
4 hundreds
3 tens
2 ones

Page 11

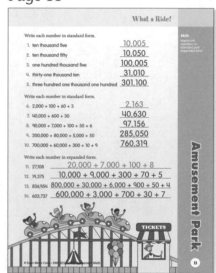

What a Ride!

Write each number in standard form.

1. ten thousand five — **10,005**
2. ten thousand fifty — **10,050**
3. one hundred thousand five — **100,005**
4. thirty-one thousand ten — **31,010**
5. three hundred one thousand one hundred — **301,100**

Write each number in standard form.

6. 2,000 + 100 + 60 + 3 — **2,163**
7. 40,000 + 600 + 30 — **40,630**
8. 90,000 + 7,000 + 100 + 50 + 6 — **97,156**
9. 200,000 + 80,000 + 5,000 + 50 — **285,050**
10. 700,000 + 60,000 + 300 + 10 + 9 — **760,319**

Write each number in expanded form.

11. 27,108 — **20,000 + 7,000 + 100 + 8**
12. 19,375 — **10,000 + 9,000 + 300 + 70 + 5**
13. 836,954 — **800,000 + 30,000 + 6,000 + 900 + 50 + 4**
14. 603,737 — **600,000 + 3,000 + 700 + 30 + 7**

Page 12

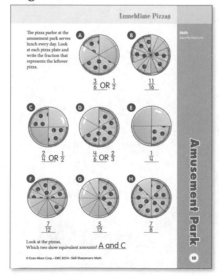

Colorful Balloons

Write > or < between the balloons to compare the two numbers.

1. 5,120 **>** 5,102
2. 6,054 **<** 6,405
3. 10,010 **>** 10,001
4. 70,193 **>** 70,139
5. 206,470 **<** 260,407
6. 330,131 **>** 303,313

7. Read the clues. Write the child's name under the correct balloon.
- The 7 in Nik's number is 100 times greater than the 7 in Claudia's number.
- The 7 in Nik's number is 10 times greater than the 7 in Yuki's number.
- The 7 in Luca's number has the least value of any of the 7s.

207,105 — **Claudia**
25,107 — **Luca**
701,520 — **Nik**
72,051 — **Yuki**

Page 13

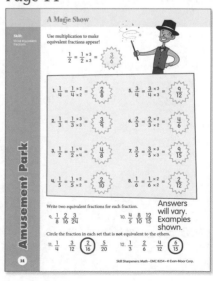

Lunchtime Pizzas

The pizza parlor at the amusement park serves lunch every day. Look at each pizza plate and write the fraction that represents the leftover pizza.

A. $\frac{3}{6}$ OR $\frac{1}{2}$
B. $\frac{11}{16}$
C. $\frac{2}{4}$ OR $\frac{1}{2}$
D. $\frac{4}{6}$ OR $\frac{2}{3}$
E. $\frac{1}{4}$
F. $\frac{7}{12}$
G. $\frac{5}{12}$
H. $\frac{7}{8}$

Look at the pizzas. Which two show equivalent amounts? **A and C**

Page 14

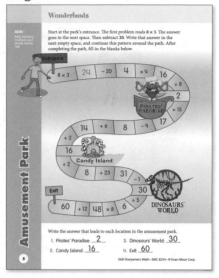

A Magic Show

Use multiplication to make equivalent fractions appear!

$$\frac{1}{2} = \frac{1 \times 3}{2 \times 3} = \frac{3}{6}$$

1. $\frac{1}{4} = \frac{1 \times 2}{4 \times 2} = \frac{2}{8}$

2. $\frac{1}{3} = \frac{1 \times 3}{3 \times 3} = \frac{3}{9}$

3. $\frac{1}{2} = \frac{1 \times 4}{2 \times 4} = \frac{4}{8}$

4. $\frac{1}{5} = \frac{1 \times 2}{5 \times 2} = \frac{2}{10}$

5. $\frac{3}{4} = \frac{3 \times 3}{4 \times 3} = \frac{9}{12}$

6. $\frac{2}{3} = \frac{2 \times 2}{3 \times 2} = \frac{4}{6}$

7. $\frac{3}{5} = \frac{3 \times 3}{5 \times 3} = \frac{9}{15}$

8. $\frac{1}{6} = \frac{1 \times 2}{6 \times 2} = \frac{2}{12}$

Write two equivalent fractions for each fraction.

Answers will vary. Examples shown.

9. $\frac{1}{8}$ — $\frac{2}{16}$ $\frac{3}{24}$

10. $\frac{4}{5}$ — $\frac{8}{10}$ $\frac{12}{15}$

Circle the fraction in each set that is not equivalent to the others.

11. $\frac{1}{4}$ $\frac{3}{12}$ Ⓐ$\frac{2}{16}$ $\frac{5}{20}$

12. $\frac{1}{3}$ $\frac{2}{6}$ $\frac{4}{12}$ Ⓐ$\frac{6}{15}$

Page 15

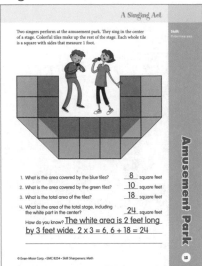

A Singing Act

Two singers perform at the amusement park. They sing in the center of a stage. Colorful tiles make up the rest of the stage. Each whole tile is a square with sides that measure 1 foot.

1. What is the area covered by the blue tiles? **8** square feet
2. What is the area covered by the green tiles? **10** square feet
3. What is the total area of the tiles? **18** square feet
4. What is the area of the total stage, including the white part in the center? **24** square feet

How do you know? **The white area is 2 feet long by 3 feet wide. 2 x 3 = 6, 6 + 18 = 24**

Amusement Park

Page 16

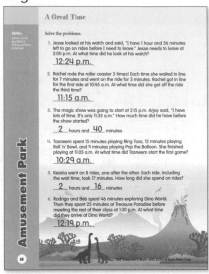

A Great Time

Solve the problems.

1. Jesse looked at his watch and said, "I have 1 hour and 36 minutes left to go on rides before I need to leave." He needs to leave at 2:00 p.m. At what time did he look at his watch?
12:24 p.m.

2. Rachel rode the roller coaster 3 times! Each time she waited in line for 7 minutes and went on the ride for 3 minutes. Rachel got in line for the first ride at 10:45 a.m. At what time did she get off the ride the third time?
11:15 a.m.

3. The magic show was going to start at 2:15 p.m. Arjay said, "I have lots of time. It's only 11:35 a.m." How much time did he have before the show started?
2 hours and **40** minutes

4. Tasneem spent 15 minutes playing Ring Toss, 12 minutes playing Roll 'n' Bowl, and 4 minutes playing Pop the Balloon. She finished playing at 11:05 a.m. At what time did Tasneem start the first game?
10:29 a.m.

5. Keisha went on 8 rides, one after the other. Each ride, including the wait time, took 17 minutes. How long did she spend on rides?
2 hours and **16** minutes

6. Rodrigo and Bob spent 46 minutes exploring Dino World. Then they spent 25 minutes at Treasure Paradise before meeting the rest of their class at 1:30 p.m. At what time did they arrive at Dino World?
12:19 p.m.

Amusement Park

Page 17

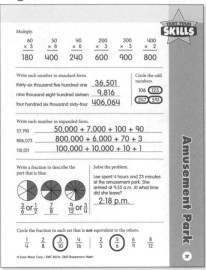

TEST YOUR SKILLS

Multiply.

60 ×3	50 ×8	40 ×6	200 ×3	300 ×3	400 ×2
180	400	240	600	900	800

Write each number in standard form.

thirty-six thousand five hundred one **36,501**
nine thousand eight hundred sixteen **9,816**
four hundred six thousand sixty-four **406,064**

Circle the odd numbers.
106 **(125)**
(247) **(591)**

Write each number in expanded form.

57,190 **50,000 + 7,000 + 100 + 90**
806,073 **800,000 + 6,000 + 70 + 3**
110,011 **100,000 + 10,000 + 10 + 1**

Write a fraction to describe the part that is blue.

3/6 or 1/2 **7/8** **9/12 or 3/4**

Solve the problem.

Lee spent 4 hours and 23 minutes at the amusement park. She arrived at 9:55 a.m. At what time did she leave?
2:18 p.m.

Circle the fraction in each set that is **not** equivalent to the others.

1/4 2/8 **(3/10)** 4/16   2/3 **(5/6)** 6/9 8/12

Amusement Park

Page 18

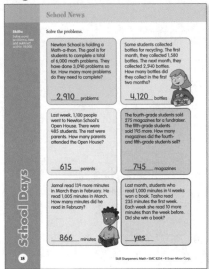

School News

Solve the problems.

Newton School is holding a Math-a-thon. The goal is for students to complete a total of 6,000 math problems. They have done 3,090 math problems so far. How many more problems do they need to complete?
2,910 problems

Some students collected bottles for recycling. The first month, they collected 1,580 bottles. The next month, they collected 2,540 bottles. How many bottles did they collect in the first two months?
4,120 bottles

Last week, 1,100 people went to Newton School's Open House. There were 485 students. The rest were parents. How many parents attended the Open House?
615 parents

The fourth-grade students sold 275 magazines for a fundraiser. The fifth-grade students sold 145 more. How many magazines did the fourth- and fifth-grade students sell?
745 magazines

Jamal read 139 more minutes in March than in February. He read 1,005 minutes in March. How many minutes did he read in February?
866 minutes

Last month, students who read 1,000 minutes in 4 weeks won a book. Tasha read 235 minutes the first week. Each week she read 10 more minutes than the week before. Did she win a book?
yes

School Days

Page 19

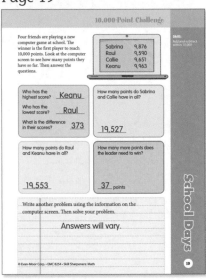

10,000-Point Challenge

Four friends are playing a new computer game at school. The winner is the first player to reach 10,000 points. Look at the computer screen to see how many points they have so far. Then answer the questions.

Sabrina	9,876
Raul	9,590
Callie	9,651
Keanu	9,963

Who has the highest score? **Keanu**
Who has the lowest score? **Raul**
What is the difference in their scores? **373**

How many points do Sabrina and Callie have in all?
19,527

How many points do Raul and Keanu have in all?
19,553

How many more points does the leader need to win?
37 points

Write another problem using the information on the computer screen. Then solve your problem.
Answers will vary.

School Days

Page 20

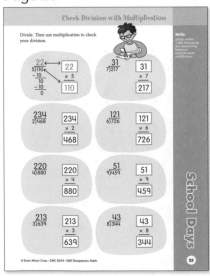

Kareem's Homework

Help Kareem with his homework.

18 ×4	12 ×5	15 ×6	12 ×7
72	60	90	84

26 ×9	59 ×7	83 ×6	74 ×8
234	413	498	592

321 ×4	106 ×6	452 ×2	216 ×6
1,284	636	904	1,296

425 ×7	316 ×6	527 ×4	411 ×9
2,975	1,896	2,108	3,699

2,013 ×6	4,252 ×2	3,042 ×6	1,124 ×4
12,078	8,504	18,252	4,496

School Days

Page 21

Figure It Out

Solve the problems.   Show Your Work

1. There are 7 classrooms. Each one has 120 textbooks. How many textbooks are there in all?
840 textbooks

2. There are 3 schools. Each school has 625 students. How many students are there altogether?
1,875 students

3. One principal holds 8 assemblies a year. Each one lasts 115 minutes. How many minutes is that in all?
920 minutes

4. A school year is made up of 180 days. Sarah went to school 6 years without missing a day. How many days was that altogether?
1,080 days

5. There are 1,247 students. Each one has 4 notebooks. How many notebooks do they have in all?
4,988 notebooks

6. Six schools each spent $3,500 for new playground equipment. How much money was spent in all?
$ **21,000**

School Days

Page 22

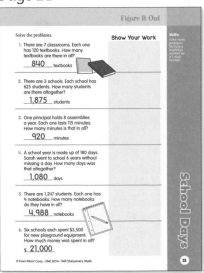

Biking to School

Write the answers on the path to help Terry get to school.

9)10 → 1
4)52 → 13
2)26 → 13
2)46 → 23
7)77 → 11
3)93 → 31
4)84 → 21
7)63 → 9
9)99 → 11
2)24 → 12
2)166 → 83
2)64 → 32
8)80 → 10
2)142 → 71
6)60 → 10
2)64 → 32
3)136 → 12
4)44 → 11
3)88 → 11
4)80 → 20
2)86 → 43

SCHOOL

School Days

Page 23

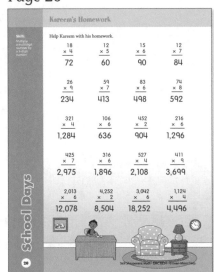

Check Division with Multiplication

Divide. Then use multiplication to check your division.

5)110 = **22**   22 × 5 = 110
7)217 = **31**   31 × 7 = 217
2)468 = **234**   234 × 2 = 468
6)726 = **121**   121 × 6 = 726
4)880 = **220**   220 × 4 = 880
9)459 = **51**   51 × 9 = 459
3)639 = **213**   213 × 3 = 639
8)344 = **43**   43 × 8 = 344

School Days

Page 24

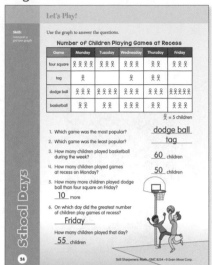

Let's Play!

Skill: Interpret a picture graph

Use the graph to answer the questions.

Number of Children Playing Games at Recess

Game	Monday	Tuesday	Wednesday	Thursday	Friday
four square	♀♀♀	♀♀	♀♀♀	♀♀	♀♀♀
tag	♀		♀	♀♀	
dodge ball	♀♀♀	♀♀♀♀	♀♀♀	♀♀♀	♀♀♀♀♀
basketball	♀♀	♀♀	♀♀♀	♀♀	♀♀♀

♀ = 5 children

1. Which game was the most popular? **dodge ball**
2. Which game was the least popular? **tag**
3. How many children played basketball during the week? **60** children
4. How many children played games at recess on Monday? **50** children
5. How many more children played dodge ball than four square on Friday? **10** more
6. On which day did the greatest number of children play games at recess? **Friday**
   How many children played that day? **55** children

School Days

Page 25

Matching Halves

Some students drew shapes in art class. The shapes below have **symmetry**. A line can be drawn on each figure so that the two halves match exactly. On some figures, more than one line can be drawn.

Draw lines of symmetry on each figure. Then write how many lines of symmetry the figure has.

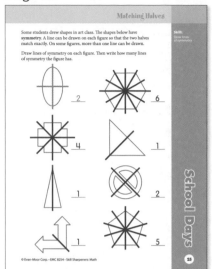

Skill: Draw lines of symmetry

School Days

Page 26

Textbook Patterns

Skill: Analyze and extend patterns

Read the rule. Then extend the pattern by writing three more numbers.

1. **Rule:** Start with 4. Add 5.
   | 4 | 9 | 14 | 19 | 24 | 29 | 34 |

   What do you notice about the numbers? **The numbers have either 4 or 9 on the end.**

2. **Rule:** Start with 3. Add 10.
   | 3 | 13 | 23 | 33 | 43 | 53 | 63 |

   What do you notice about the numbers? **The numbers end in 3. The numbers are odd.**

3. **Rule:** Start with 100. Subtract 2.
   | 100 | 98 | 96 | 94 | 92 | 90 | 88 |

   What do you notice about the numbers? **The numbers are even and are getting smaller.**

4. **Rule:** Start with 90. Subtract 9.
   | 90 | 81 | 72 | 63 | 54 | 45 | 36 |

   What do you notice about the numbers? **They are multiples of 9. Their digits add up to 9.**

School Days

Page 27

Fractions and Number Lines

Skill: Compare fractions

You can use a number line to compare fractions.

Example: Compare $\frac{3}{10}$ and $\frac{3}{4}$.

Plot each fraction on the number line. Use the fraction $\frac{1}{2}$ to help you. $\frac{3}{10}$ is less than $\frac{1}{2}$ and $\frac{3}{4}$ is greater than $\frac{1}{2}$.

$\frac{3}{10}$ < $\frac{3}{4}$

Plot the fractions on the number line. Write >, <, or = to compare the fractions.

1. $\frac{3}{5}$ $\frac{3}{8}$ $\frac{3}{5}$ > $\frac{3}{8}$
2. $\frac{1}{4}$ $\frac{2}{3}$ $\frac{1}{4}$ < $\frac{2}{3}$
3. $\frac{5}{6}$ $\frac{5}{10}$ $\frac{5}{10}$ < $\frac{5}{6}$
4. $\frac{6}{8}$ $\frac{3}{4}$ $\frac{3}{4}$ = $\frac{6}{8}$

5. Kai lives $\frac{4}{5}$ mile from school. Joy lives $\frac{4}{8}$ mile from school. Who lives farther from school? How do you know?
   Kai. $\frac{4}{5}$ is almost a mile. $\frac{4}{8}$ is only half.

School Days

Page 28

Science Class

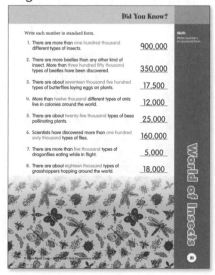

Skills: Convert measurements (metric units); Determine area and perimeter

Use the information in the box to help you solve the problems.

Metric Units of Length
10 millimeters (mm) = 1 centimeter (cm)
100 centimeters = 1 meter (m)
1,000 meters = 1 kilometer (km)

1. Mrs. Kami's students measured their shadows at 9:00 a.m. and at noon. Megan's shadow was 85 cm longer at 9:00 than at noon.
   Megan's shadow at noon was 135 centimeters long. How long was it at 9:00? **220 cm**
   Was her 9:00 shadow longer than or shorter than 2 meters? **longer**

2. Mr. Franklin's students tested how far their paper airplanes flew. Vanessa's plane flew 620 centimeters. Shawn's plane flew 6$\frac{1}{2}$ meters.
   Whose plane flew farther? **Shawn's**
   How much farther did that plane fly? **30 cm**

3. [illegible] threadsnake is [illegible].
   How many millimeters is that? **100 mm**
   Is it longer or shorter than a garter snake that is a half meter long? **shorter**

4. Jayden made a poster to advertise the science fair. The poster was 2 meters tall and 1 meter wide. What was its perimeter in meters, centimeters, and millimeters?
   6 m   **600** cm   **6,000** mm

School Days

Page 29

On the Map

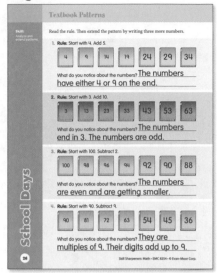

Skill: Measure length in centimeters

This map represents the western half of the United States.

Use a centimeter ruler to measure distances to the nearest centimeter. Write the measurements. Then use them to answer the questions about distance.

Map Scale
1 cm = 250 km

1. Measure the distance from Dallas, Texas, to Denver, Colorado. About how many kilometers is it from Dallas to Denver?
   4 cm   **1,000** km

2. [illegible] from Butte to Dallas, Texas. About how many kilometers is it from Butte to Dallas?
   8 cm   **2,000** km

3. Measure the distance from San Diego, California, to Boise, Idaho. About how many kilometers is it from San Diego to Boise?
   5 cm   **1,250** km

4. Measure the distance from Phoenix, Arizona, to San Diego, California. About how many kilometers is it from Phoenix to San Diego?
   2 cm   **500** km

School Days

Page 30

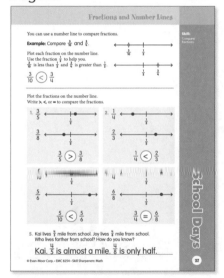

TEST YOUR SKILLS

Add or subtract.

4,612	5,873	9,580	6,000
+ 3,209	+ 2,456	− 3,177	− 1,248
7,821	8,329	6,403	4,752

Multiply or divide.

26	53	183	3,272
× 8	× 7	× 8	× 5
208	371	1,464	16,360

18	34	170	129
4)72	2)68	5)850	7)903

Plot the fractions on the number line. Write >, <, or = to compare the fractions.

$\frac{3}{8}$ $\frac{3}{4}$ $\frac{3}{8}$ < $\frac{3}{4}$

Draw a line of symmetry on the figure.

Mia is 140 centimeters tall. Kasey is 1$\frac{1}{2}$ meters tall. Who is taller? How many centimeters taller?
Kasey **10** cm taller

School Days

Page 31

Did You Know?

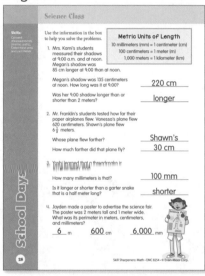

Skill: Write numbers in standard form

Write each number in standard form.

1. There are more than nine hundred thousand different types of insects. **900,000**
2. There are more beetles than any other kind of insect. More than three hundred fifty thousand types of beetles have been discovered. **350,000**
3. There are about seventeen thousand five hundred types of butterflies laying eggs on plants. **17,500**
4. More than twelve thousand different types of ants live in colonies around the world. **12,000**
5. There are about twenty-five thousand types of bees pollinating plants. **25,000**
6. Scientists have discovered more than one hundred sixty thousand types of flies. **160,000**
7. There are more than five thousand types of dragonflies eating insects while in flight. **5,000**
8. There are about eighteen thousand types of grasshoppers hopping around the world. **18,000**

World of Insects

Page 32

Leafy Numbers

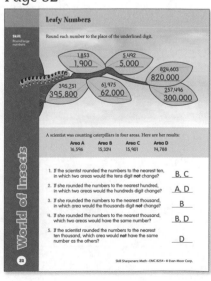

Skill: Round large numbers

Round each number to the place of the underlined digit.

1,853 → 1,900
5,492 → 5,000
824,603 → 820,000
395,751 → 395,800
61,975 → 62,000
257,496 → 300,000

A scientist was counting caterpillars in four areas. Here are her results:

Area A	Area B	Area C	Area D
16,596	15,324	15,901	14,788

1. If the scientist rounded the numbers to the nearest ten, in which two areas would the tens digit **not** change? **B, C**
2. If she rounded the numbers to the nearest hundred, in which two areas would the hundreds digit change? **A, D**
3. If she rounded the numbers to the nearest thousand, in which area would the thousands digit **not** change? **B**
4. If she rounded the numbers to the nearest thousand, which two areas would have the same number? **B, D**
5. If the scientist rounded the numbers to the nearest ten thousand, which area would have the same number as the others? **D**

World of Insects

Page 33

Making Large Numbers Simple

Skill: Round large numbers

Round each number to the place value listed.
1. 7,465 (hundreds) — 7,500
2. 14,309 (tens) — 14,310
3. 28,731 (thousands) — 29,000
4. 590,472 (ten thousands) — 590,000
5. 289,962 (hundred thousands) — 300,000
6. 190,749 (tens) — 190,750
7. 83,802 (hundreds) — 83,800
8. 730,801 (thousands) — 731,000
9. 69,730 (ten thousands) — 70,000
10. 287,521 (thousands) — 288,000

Round the number **420,694** to the place values listed.
11. tens — 420,690
12. hundreds — 420,700
13. thousands — 421,000
14. ten thousands — 420,000
15. hundred thousands — 400,000

World of Insects

Page 34

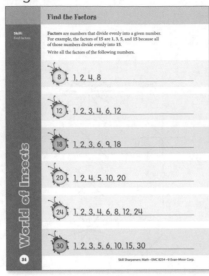

Find the Factors

Skill: Find factors

Factors are numbers that divide evenly into a given number. For example, the factors of **15** are 1, 3, 5, and 15 because all of those numbers divide evenly into 15.

Write all the factors of the following numbers.

8 — 1, 2, 4, 8
12 — 1, 2, 3, 4, 6, 12
18 — 1, 2, 3, 6, 9, 18
20 — 1, 2, 4, 5, 10, 20
24 — 1, 2, 3, 4, 6, 8, 12, 24
30 — 1, 2, 3, 5, 6, 10, 15, 30

World of Insects

Page 35

Hunt for Primes

Skill: Identify prime and composite numbers

- Circle all prime numbers in red.
- Cross out all the composite numbers in blue.

Prime numbers have exactly two factors: **1** and the number itself. *Example: 2 (factors = 1 and 2)*

Composite numbers have more than two factors. They are multiples of other numbers. *Example: 4 (factors = 1, 2, 4)*

The first prime number and the first composite number have been marked for you. The number 1 is blocked out because it is neither prime nor composite.

World of Insects

Page 36

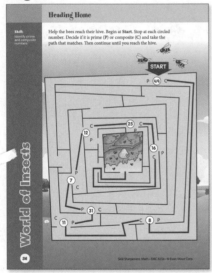

Heading Home

Skill: Identify prime and composite numbers

Help the bees reach their hive. Begin at **Start**. Stop at each circled number. Decide if it is prime (P) or composite (C) and take the path that matches. Then continue until you reach the hive.

World of Insects

Page 37

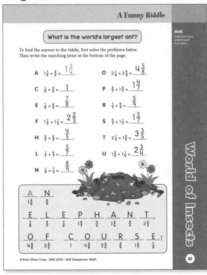

A Funny Riddle

Skill: Add fractions and mixed numbers

What is the world's largest ant?

To find the answer to the riddle, first solve the problems below. Then write the matching letter at the bottom of the page.

A $1\frac{1}{4} + \frac{1}{2} = 1\frac{3}{4}$
C $\frac{1}{4} + \frac{3}{4} = 1$
E $\frac{1}{8} + \frac{3}{4} = \frac{7}{8}$
F $1\frac{1}{3} + 1\frac{1}{3} = 2\frac{2}{3}$
H $\frac{3}{5} + \frac{1}{5} = \frac{4}{5}$
L $\frac{1}{7} + \frac{4}{7} = \frac{5}{7}$
N $\frac{1}{4} + \frac{4}{4} = \frac{8}{9}$

O $2\frac{1}{8} + 2\frac{1}{2} = 4\frac{5}{8}$
P $\frac{7}{9} + 1\frac{1}{2} = 1\frac{7}{9}$
R $\frac{1}{6} + \frac{4}{6} = \frac{5}{9}$
S $\frac{4}{7} + 1\frac{1}{7} = 1\frac{5}{7}$
T $2\frac{1}{5} + 1\frac{2}{5} = 3\frac{3}{5}$
U $1\frac{4}{9} + 1\frac{1}{4} = 2\frac{3}{4}$

A N   E L E P H A N T   O F   C O U R S E !

World of Insects

Page 38

Bee Careful!

Skill: Subtract fractions and mixed numbers

Solve the problems.
1. $\frac{5}{8} - \frac{1}{3} = \frac{1}{3}$
2. $\frac{4}{7} - \frac{1}{7} = \frac{5}{7}$
3. $\frac{5}{8} - \frac{3}{8} = \frac{1}{4}$
4. $\frac{8}{9} - \frac{1}{9} = \frac{7}{9}$
5. $\frac{4}{5} - \frac{2}{5} = \frac{2}{5}$
6. $\frac{6}{7} - \frac{3}{7} = \frac{3}{7}$
7. $\frac{7}{8} - \frac{4}{8} = \frac{1}{8}$
8. $\frac{5}{6} - \frac{4}{6} = \frac{1}{6}$
9. $\frac{9}{10} - \frac{2}{10} = \frac{7}{10}$
10. $\frac{6}{9} - \frac{4}{9} = \frac{2}{9}$
11. $6\frac{3}{4} - 1\frac{1}{2} = 5\frac{2}{4}$ OR $5\frac{1}{2}$
12. $5\frac{7}{9} - 1\frac{5}{9} = 4\frac{2}{9}$
13. $6\frac{4}{7} - 2\frac{1}{7} = 4\frac{5}{7}$
14. $5\frac{3}{5} - 2\frac{3}{5} = 3\frac{3}{5}$
15. $8\frac{7}{8} - 5\frac{4}{8} = 3\frac{1}{8}$
16. $4\frac{5}{10} - 2\frac{4}{10} = 2\frac{3}{10}$

World of Insects

Page 39

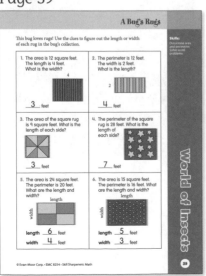

A Bug's Rugs

Skills: Determine area and perimeter; Solve word problems.

This bug loves rugs! Use the clues to figure out the length or width of each rug in the bug's collection.

1. The area is 12 square feet. The length is 4 feet. What is the width? — 3 feet
2. The perimeter is 12 feet. The width is 2 feet. What is the length? — 4 feet
3. The area of the square rug is 9 square feet. What is the length of each side? — 3 feet
4. The perimeter of the square rug is 28 feet. What is the length of each side? — 7 feet
5. The area is 24 square feet. The perimeter is 20 feet. What are the length and width? — length 6 feet, width 4 feet
6. The area is 15 square feet. The perimeter is 16 feet. What are the length and width? — length 5 feet, width 3 feet

World of Insects

Page 40

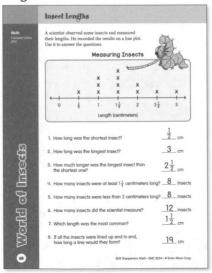

Insect Lengths

Skill: Interpret a line plot.

A scientist observed some insects and measured their lengths. He recorded the results on a line plot. Use it to answer the questions.

Measuring Insects

Length (centimeters)

1. How long was the shortest insect? — $\frac{1}{2}$ cm
2. How long was the longest insect? — 3 cm
3. How much longer was the longest insect than the shortest one? — $2\frac{1}{2}$ cm
4. How many insects were at least $1\frac{1}{2}$ centimeters long? — 8 insects
5. How many insects were less than 2 centimeters long? — 8 insects
6. How many insects did the scientist measure? — 12 insects
7. Which length was the most common? — $1\frac{1}{2}$ cm
8. If all the insects were lined up end to end, how long a line would they form? — 19 cm

World of Insects

Page 41

Butterfly Symmetry

Skill: Draw symmetrical shapes

Butterflies have a symmetrical shape and pattern. Each half of the butterfly matches the other. Draw the missing half of each butterfly and color it. For the last two butterflies, draw your own amazing patterns!

Drawings will vary.

World of Insects

Page 42

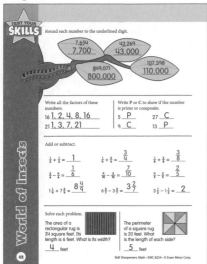

TEST YOUR SKILLS

Round each number to the underlined digit.

7,654 → 7,700
43,269 → 43,000
107,398 → 110,000
849,071 → 800,000

Write all the factors of these numbers.
16 1, 2, 4, 8, 16
21 1, 3, 7, 21

Write P or C to show if the number is prime or composite.
5 P   27 C
9 C   13 P

Add or subtract.
$\frac{1}{2} + \frac{1}{2} = 1$ $\frac{1}{4} + \frac{2}{4} = \frac{3}{4}$ $\frac{1}{4} + \frac{2}{8} = \frac{3}{8}$
$\frac{3}{4} - \frac{4}{8} = \frac{1}{6}$ $\frac{9}{10} - \frac{2}{10} = \frac{7}{10}$ $\frac{4}{5} - \frac{2}{5} = \frac{2}{5}$
$1\frac{1}{4} + 7\frac{3}{4} = 8\frac{4}{9}$ $6\frac{3}{7} - 3\frac{1}{7} = 3\frac{2}{7}$ $3\frac{1}{2} - 1\frac{1}{2} = 2$

Solve each problem.

The area of a rectangular rug is 24 square feet. Its length is 6 feet. What is its width?
4 feet

The perimeter of a square rug is 20 feet. What is the length of each side?
5 feet

World of Insects

Page 43

Cookie Puzzler

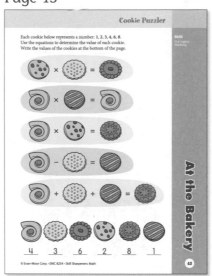

Each cookie below represents a number: 1, 2, 3, 4, 6, 8. Use the equations to determine the value of each cookie. Write the values of the cookies at the bottom of the page.

4   3   6   2   8   1

At the Bakery

Page 44

Best-Selling Bread

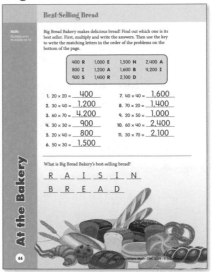

Big Bread Bakery makes delicious bread! Find out which one is its best seller. First, multiply and write the answers. Then use the key to write the matching letters in the order of the problems on the bottom of the page.

400 R	1,000 E	1,500 N	2,400 A
800 I	1,200 A	1,600 B	4,200 I
900 S	1,400 R	2,100 D	

1. 20 × 20 = 400
2. 30 × 40 = 1,200
3. 60 × 70 = 4,200
4. 30 × 30 = 900
5. 20 × 40 = 800
6. 50 × 30 = 1,500
7. 40 × 40 = 1,600
8. 70 × 20 = 1,400
9. 20 × 50 = 1,000
10. 60 × 40 = 2,400
11. 30 × 70 = 2,100

What is Big Bread Bakery's best-selling bread?
R A I S I N   B R E A D

At the Bakery

Page 45

Muffin Multiplication

Multiply.

24 × 20 = 480   13 × 30 = 390   31 × 50 = 550   42 × 40 = 1,680
93 × 40 = 3,720   68 × 20 = 1,360   19 × 70 = 1,330   36 × 40 = 1,440
57 × 60 = 3,420   91 × 90 = 8,190   83 × 30 = 2,490   65 × 50 = 3,250

How will knowing 62 × 3 help you solve 62 × 30?
Answers may vary. Example shown.
62 × 30 is 10 times larger than 62 × 3. To find 62 × 30, you can multiply 62 × 3 and add a 0 at the end of the product.

At the Bakery

Page 46

Bakery Buys

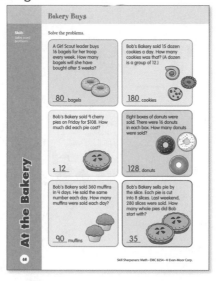

Solve the problems.

A Girl Scout leader buys 16 bagels for her troop every week. How many bagels will she have bought after 5 weeks?
80 bagels

Bob's Bakery sold 15 dozen cookies a day. How many cookies was that? (A dozen is a group of 12.)
180 cookies

Bob's Bakery sold 9 cherry pies on Friday for $108. How much did each pie cost?
$12

Eight boxes of donuts were sold. There were 16 donuts in each box. How many donuts were sold?
128 donuts

Bob's Bakery sold 360 muffins in 4 days. He sold the same number each day. How many muffins were sold each day?
90 muffins

Bob's Bakery sells pie by the slice. Each pie is cut into 8 slices. Last weekend, 280 slices were sold. How many whole pies did Bob start with?
35

At the Bakery

Page 47

Finding Multiples

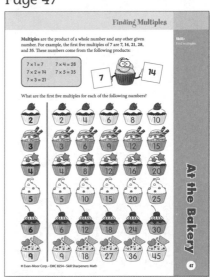

Multiples are the product of a whole number and any other given number. For example, the first five multiples of 7 are 7, 14, 21, 28, and 35. These numbers come from the following products:

7 × 1 = 7   7 × 4 = 28
7 × 2 = 14   7 × 5 = 35
7 × 3 = 21

7   14

What are the first five multiples of each of the following numbers?

2   2 4 6 8 10
3   3 6 9 12 15
4   4 8 12 16 20
5   5 10 15 20 25
6   6 12 18 24 30
9   9 18 27 36 45

At the Bakery

Page 48

A Grand Opening

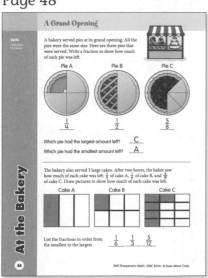

A bakery served pies at its grand opening. All the pies were the same size. Here are three pies that were served. Write a fraction to show how much of each pie was left.

Pie A: $\frac{1}{4}$ Pie B: $\frac{1}{2}$ Pie C: $\frac{5}{8}$

Which pie had the largest amount left? C
Which pie had the smallest amount left? A

The bakery also served 3 large cakes. After two hours, the baker saw how much of each cake was left: $\frac{1}{3}$ of cake A, $\frac{1}{6}$ of cake B, and $\frac{5}{12}$ of cake C. Draw pictures to show how much of each cake was left.

Cake A   Cake B   Cake C

List the fractions in order from the smallest to the largest.
$\frac{1}{6}$ $\frac{1}{3}$ $\frac{5}{12}$

At the Bakery

Page 49

Recipe Measures

Solve the problems. Write your answers as whole numbers or mixed numbers.

1. A baker made 7 batches of cookies. She used $\frac{1}{2}$ teaspoon of salt for each batch. How many teaspoons of salt did she use in all?
$3\frac{1}{2}$ teaspoons

$7 \times \frac{1}{2} = \frac{7}{2}$
$= 3\frac{1}{2}$

2. A brownie recipe calls for $\frac{3}{4}$ cup of flour. The recipe makes 16 brownies. How much flour is needed for 48 brownies?
$2\frac{1}{4}$ cups OR $\frac{9}{4}$

3. It takes $\frac{1}{3}$ cup of sour cream to make 1 loaf of lemon bread. A baker made 6 loaves of lemon bread. How many cups of sour cream did he use?
2 cups

4. It takes $\frac{1}{4}$ cup of butter to make 1 batch of biscuits. How many cups of butter are needed for 5 batches?
$1\frac{1}{4}$ cups OR $\frac{5}{4}$

5. An apple pie recipe calls for $\frac{1}{8}$ teaspoon of nutmeg. How much nutmeg is needed for 15 apple pies?
$1\frac{7}{8}$ teaspoons OR $\frac{15}{8}$

At the Bakery

Page 50

Cake Candles

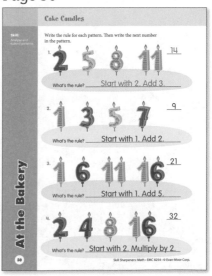

Write the rule for each pattern. Then write the next number in the pattern.

1. 2 5 8 11 14
What's the rule? Start with 2. Add 3.

2. 1 3 5 7 9
What's the rule? Start with 1. Add 2.

3. 1 6 11 16 21
What's the rule? Start with 1. Add 5.

4. 2 4 8 16 32
What's the rule? Start with 2. Multiply by 2.

At the Bakery

Page 51

Cool Cupcakes

Every day, a bakery displayed cupcakes in long rows.
Read the clues and answer the questions.

Skills:
Analyze patterns;
Find common
factors

1. On Monday, there were 24 cupcakes.
Every 2nd cupcake was purple.
Every 3rd cupcake had sprinkles.

   How many cupcakes were purple? **12**

   How many cupcakes had sprinkles? **8**

   How many cupcakes were purple **and** had sprinkles? **4**

2. On Tuesday, there were 40 cupcakes.
Every 4th cupcake had vanilla icing.
Every 5th cupcake had a cherry on top.

   How many cupcakes had vanilla icing? **10**

   How many cupcakes had a cherry on top? **8**

   How many cupcakes had vanilla icing **and** a cherry? **2**

3. On Wednesday, there were 36 cupcakes.
Every 3rd cupcake was chocolate. Every
6th cupcake had candy stars.

   How many cupcakes were chocolate? **12**

   How many cupcakes had candy stars? **6**

   How many chocolate cupcakes **also** had candy stars? **6**

At the Bakery

© Evan-Moor Corp. • EMC 8254 • Skill Sharpeners: Math · 51

Page 52

Skill:
Uncover
measurements;
U.S. customary
units of weight

Bakery Weights

Use the information
in the box to help you
solve the problems.

U.S. Customary Units of Weight
16 ounces (oz) = 1 pound (lb)

1. A baker used 5 pounds of flour to make several
loaves of bread. How many ounces of flour did
the baker use? **80** oz

2. A cake weighed 48 ounces. How many pounds
did it weigh? **3** lb

3. Which weighs more—30 ounces of white sugar
or 2 pounds of brown sugar? How much more?
brown sugar **2** oz more

4. A loaf of bread weighed 24 ounces. Is that
greater than, less than, or equal to 1½ pounds?
equal to

5. An 8-ounce bag of pretzel sticks sells for $2.00.
How much would 1½ pounds of pretzel sticks cost? $ **6.00**

6. A large cake weighed 20 pounds and served
100 people. How many pounds would half the
cake weigh? **10** lb

   How many ounces is that? **160** oz

At the Bakery

52 · Skill Sharpeners: Math • EMC 8254 • © Evan-Moor Corp.

Page 53

Perfect Pies

Perfect Pies Bakery sells different pies for different prices. Read the
clues and fill in the table to match each pie with its price. When you
know that a pie and a price do **not** go together, make an X under that
price and across from that pie. When you know that a pie and a price
do go together, write YES in that box.

Skill:
Use logical
reasoning

Clues
- The apple pie is not the most expensive pie.
- The lemon pie costs more than the cherry pie.
- The blueberry pie costs more than $12.
- The strawberry pie costs more than the blueberry pie.
- The cherry pie is not the least expensive pie.

	$8	$10	$12	$14	$16
apple	yes	X	X	X	X
blueberry	X	X	X	yes	X
strawberry	X	X	X	X	yes
lemon	X	X	yes	X	X
cherry	X	yes	X	X	X

Write the price beside the matching pie.

apple $ **8**   lemon $ **12**

blueberry $ **14**   cherry $ **10**

strawberry $ **16**

At the Bakery

© Evan-Moor Corp. • EMC 8254 • Skill Sharpeners: Math · 53

Page 54

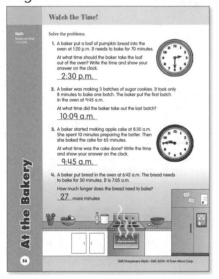

Skill:
Measure time
intervals

Watch the Time!

Solve the problems.

1. A baker put a loaf of pumpkin bread into the
oven at 1:20 p.m. It needs to bake for 70 minutes.
At what time should the baker take the loaf
out of the oven? Write the time and show your
answer on the clock.
2:30 p.m.

2. A baker was making 3 batches of sugar cookies. It took only
8 minutes to bake one batch. The baker put the first batch
in the oven at 9:45 a.m.
At what time did the baker take out the last batch?
10:09 a.m.

3. A baker started making apple cake at 8:30 a.m.
She spent 10 minutes preparing the batter. Then
she baked the cake for 65 minutes.
At what time was the cake done? Write the time
and show your answer on the clock.
9:45 a.m.

4. A baker put bread in the oven at 6:42 a.m. The bread needs
to bake for 50 minutes. It is 7:05 a.m.
How much longer does the bread need to bake?
27 more minutes

At the Bakery

54 · Skill Sharpeners: Math • EMC 8254 • © Evan-Moor Corp.

Page 55

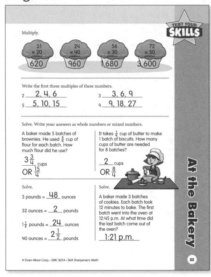

TEST YOUR SKILLS

Multiply.

31 × 20	24 × 40	56 × 30	72 × 50
620	960	1,680	3,600

Write the first three multiples of these numbers.

2 **2, 4, 6**   3 **3, 6, 9**

5 **5, 10, 15**   9 **9, 18, 27**

Solve. Write your answers as whole numbers or mixed numbers.

A baker made 5 batches of
brownies. He used ¾ cup of
flour for each batch. How
much flour did he use?
3 ¾ cups
OR **15/4**

It takes ¼ cup of butter to make
1 batch of biscuits. How many
cups of butter are needed
for 8 batches?
2 cups
OR **8/4**

Solve.

3 pounds = **48** ounces

32 ounces = **2** pounds

1½ pounds = **24** ounces

40 ounces = **2 ½** pounds

Solve.

A baker made 3 batches
of cookies. Each batch took
12 minutes to bake. The first
batch went into the oven at
12:45 p.m. At what time did
the last batch come out of
the oven?
1:21 p.m.

At the Bakery

© Evan-Moor Corp. • EMC 8254 • Skill Sharpeners: Math · 55

Page 56

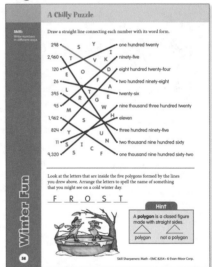

A Chilly Puzzle

Skill:
Write numbers
in different ways

Draw a straight line connecting each number with its word form.

298   one hundred twenty

2,960   ninety-five

120   eight hundred twenty-four

26   two hundred ninety-eight

395   twenty-six

95   nine thousand three hundred twenty

1,962   eleven

824   three hundred ninety-five

11   two thousand nine hundred sixty

9,320   one thousand nine hundred sixty-two

Look at the letters that are inside the five polygons formed by the lines
you drew above. Arrange the letters to spell the name of something
that you might see on a cold winter day.

F R O S T

Hint
A **polygon** is a closed figure
made with straight sides.

polygon   not a polygon

Winter Fun

56 · Skill Sharpeners: Math • EMC 8254 • © Evan-Moor Corp.

Page 57

A Snowy Hill

Multiply.

Skill:
Multiply
multidigit
numbers

43 × 21	32 × 23	27 × 34	25 × 25
903	736	918	625

17 × 16	23 × 42	39 × 31	62 × 25
272	966	1,209	1,550

57 × 52	82 × 24	76 × 37	94 × 42
2,964	1,968	2,812	3,948

37 × 47	78 × 59	65 × 47
1,739	4,602	3,055

Winter Fun

© Evan-Moor Corp. • EMC 8254 • Skill Sharpeners: Math · 57

Page 58

A Winter Tongue Twister

Skill:
Divide with
remainders

Solve the division problems. Then write the letter from the code
for each remainder to make a tongue twister. Try saying the
phrase quickly three times!

Remainder Code
1 E	5 O
2 I	6 S
3 M	7 W
4 N	8 X

34 ÷ 7 = **4** remainder of **6** **S**

20 ÷ 6 = **3** remainder of **2** **I**

80 ÷ 9 = **8** remainder of **8** **X**

54 ÷ 8 = **6** remainder of **6** **S**

49 ÷ 5 = **9** remainder of **4** **N**

35 ÷ 6 = **5** remainder of **5** **O**

43 ÷ 9 = **4** remainder of **7** **W**

39 ÷ 4 = **9** remainder of **3** **M**

50 ÷ 7 = **7** remainder of **1** **E**

68 ÷ 8 = **8** remainder of **4** **N**

Winter Fun

58 · Skill Sharpeners: Math • EMC 8254 • © Evan-Moor Corp.

Page 59

Let It Snow!

Solve the division problems.

Skill:
Divide with
remainders

10 R2 4)42	9 R5 6)59	9 R1 3)28	8 R3 9)75

11 R6 7)83	18 R3 5)93	21 R3 4)87	32 R2 3)98

124 R1 2)249	223 R1 4)893	328 R2 3)986	134 R4 5)674

Winter Fun

© Evan-Moor Corp. • EMC 8254 • Skill Sharpeners: Math · 59

Page 60
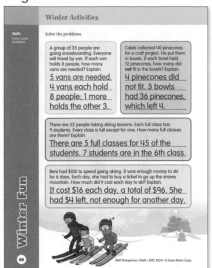

Page 61
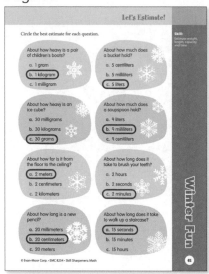

Page 62
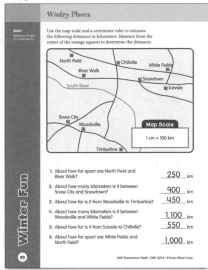

Page 63
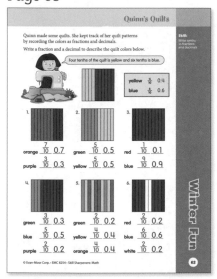

Page 64
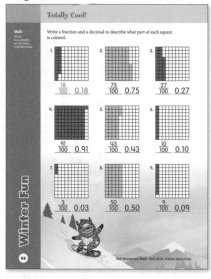

Page 65
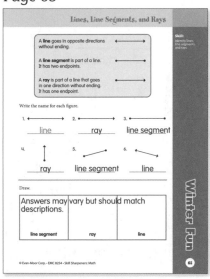

Page 66
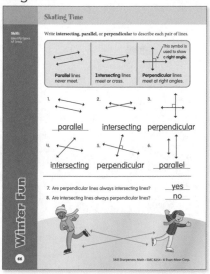

Page 67
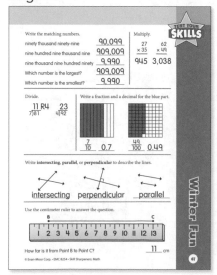

Page 68
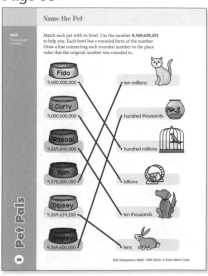

Page 69

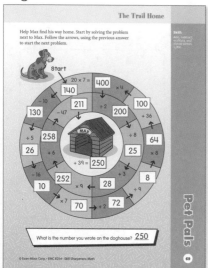

The Trail Home

Help Max find his way home. Start by solving the problem next to Max. Follow the arrows, using the previous answer to start the next problem.

Start

20 × 7 = **400**

140 ×4

130 −10 **211** ÷2 **200** **100** +36

÷5 **258** **64** ÷8

26 +6 **25** ×8

10 −16 **252** **8** ÷3

70 ×7 **28** ×9 **72** ÷9

+39 = **250**

What is the number you wrote on the doghouse? **250**

© Evan-Moor Corp. • EMC 8254 • Skill Sharpeners: Math

69

Pet Pals

Page 70

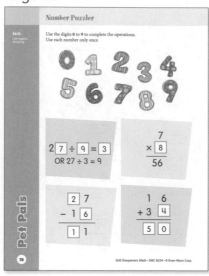

Number Puzzler

Use the digits **0** to **9** to complete the operations. Use each number only once.

0 1 2 3 4
5 6 7 8 9

2 7 ÷ 9 = 3
OR 27 ÷ 3 = 9

7
× 8
56

2 7
− 1 6
1 1

1 6
+ 3 4
5 0

Skill Sharpeners: Math • EMC 8254 • © Evan-Moor Corp.

70

Pet Pals

Page 71

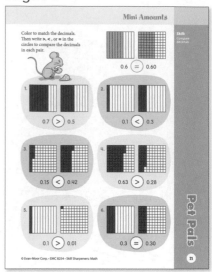

Mini Amounts

Color to match the decimals. Then write >, <, or = in the circles to compare the decimals in each pair.

0.6 = 0.60

1. 0.7 > 0.5   2. 0.1 < 0.3

3. 0.15 < 0.42   4. 0.63 > 0.28

5. 0.1 > 0.01   6. 0.3 = 0.30

© Evan-Moor Corp. • EMC 8254 • Skill Sharpeners: Math

71

Pet Pals

Page 72

A Funny Pet Riddle

What pet goes ticktock, woof woof?

To find the answer to the riddle, first solve each problem. Then write the letter on each line above the matching sum.

A 0.5 + 0.3 = **0.8**
A 0.4 + 0.2 = **0.6**
C 0.25 + 0.52 = **0.77**
D 4.0 + 0.2 = **4.2**
G 0.5 + 3.0 = **3.5**
H 0.3 + 0.27 = **0.57**
O 2.5 + 0.52 = **3.02**
T 0.25 + 5.2 = **5.45**
W 0.52 + 0.71 = **1.23**

ticktock   woof woof

A W A T C H
0.6 1.23 0.8 5.45 0.77 0.57

D O G
4.2 3.02 3.5

72

Skill Sharpeners: Math • EMC 8254 • © Evan-Moor Corp.

Pet Pals

Page 73

Tongue Twister Challenge

Solve the problems. Then write the letter for each answer on the matching line below. Try saying the tongue twister quickly three times!

A 5.3 − 1.2 = 1.3
D 5.3 − 2.1 = 3.2
E 4.6 − 1.3 = 3.3
H 9.5 − 8.4 = 1.1

I 5.2 − 4.8 = 0.4
K 4.12 − 3.09 = 1.03
L 5.26 − 4.13 = 1.13
N 8.69 − 1.26 = 7.43

R 6.49 − 5.2 = 1.29
S 7.25 − 4.1 = 3.15
T 5.5 − 1.26 = 4.24

V 8.24 − 7.03 = 1.21
Y 4.81 − 3.07 = 1.74

S E V E N S I L L Y
3.15 3.3 1.21 3.3 7.43 3.15 0.4 1.13 1.13 1.74

S N A K E S
3.15 7.43 1.3 1.03 3.3 3.15

S L I T H E R E D
3.15 1.13 0.4 4.24 1.1 3.3 1.29 3.3 3.2

© Evan-Moor Corp. • EMC 8254 • Skill Sharpeners: Math

73

Pet Pals

Page 74

At the Pet Store

Solve the problems.

Amir went to the pet store to buy birdseed. The food cost $2.94. Amir paid with a $5.00 bill. How much change did he get back?

$ **2.06**

Kiana bought her dog a leash and a collar. The leash cost $4.75 and the collar cost $6.50. Kiana paid with a $20.00 bill. How much change did she get back?

$ **8.75**

A neon tetra is a small aquarium fish. One store is selling them for $1.60 each. If Seth has a $10.00 bill, how many neon tetras can he buy?

6 fish

Lara bought the wrong kind of turtle food. The store gives her a refund of $5.70. The new food that she buys costs $10.25. She uses her refund to pay for part of the new food. How much more does she need to pay?

$ **4.55**

Toshi will buy 3 cat toys for $1.92 each. If he pays in dollar bills, how many will he need?

6 dollar bills

How much change will he receive? $ **0.24**

74

Skill Sharpeners: Math • EMC 8254 • © Evan-Moor Corp.

Pet Pals

Page 75

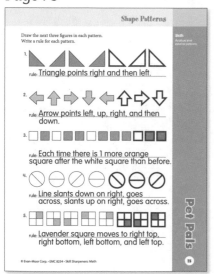

Shape Patterns

Draw the next three figures in each pattern. Write a rule for each pattern.

1.
rule: Triangle points right and then left.

2.
rule: Arrow points left, up, right, and then down.

3.
rule: Each time there is 1 more orange square after the white square than before.

4.
rule: Line slants down on right, goes across, slants up on right, goes across.

5.
rule: Lavender square moves to right top, right bottom, left bottom, and left top.

© Evan-Moor Corp. • EMC 8254 • Skill Sharpeners: Math

75

Pet Pals

Page 76

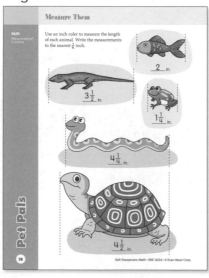

Measure Them

Use an inch ruler to measure the length of each animal. Write the measurements to the nearest $\frac{1}{4}$ inch.

_2_ in.

$3\frac{1}{2}$ in.

$1\frac{1}{4}$ in.

$4\frac{1}{4}$ in.

$4\frac{1}{2}$ in.

76

Skill Sharpeners: Math • EMC 8254 • © Evan-Moor Corp.

Pet Pals

Page 77

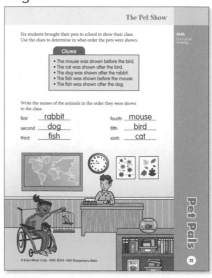

The Pet Show

Six students brought their pets to school to show their class. Use the clues to determine in what order the pets were shown.

Clues
- The mouse was shown before the bird.
- The cat was shown after the bird.
- The dog was shown after the rabbit.
- The fish was shown before the mouse.
- The fish was shown after the dog.

Write the names of the animals in the order they were shown to the class.

first rabbit   fourth mouse
second dog   fifth bird
third fish   sixth cat

© Evan-Moor Corp. • EMC 8254 • Skill Sharpeners: Math

77

Pet Pals

Page 78

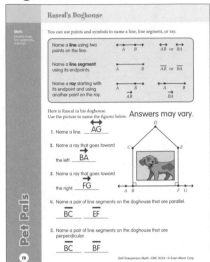

Page 79

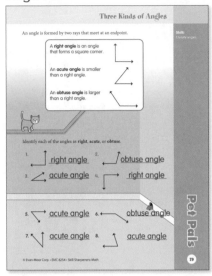

Page 80

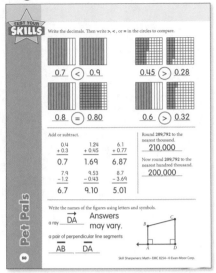

Page 81

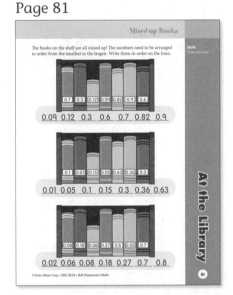

Page 82

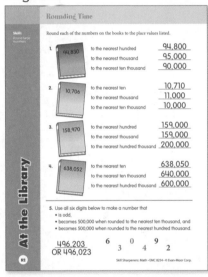

Page 83

Page 84

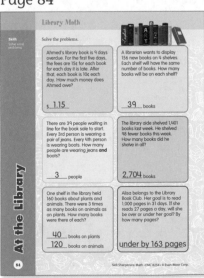

Page 85

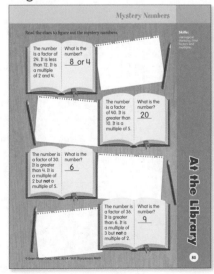

Page 86

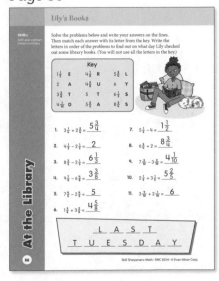

Page 87

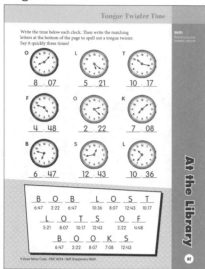

Page 88

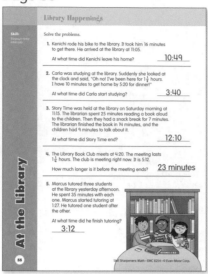

Page 89

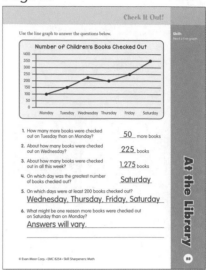

Page 90

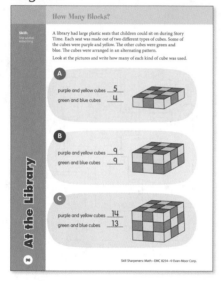

Page 91

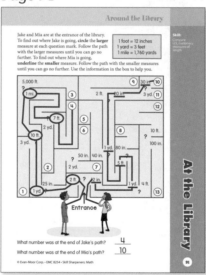

Page 92

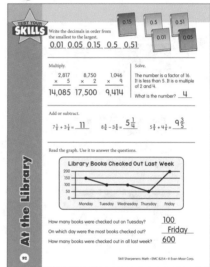

Page 93

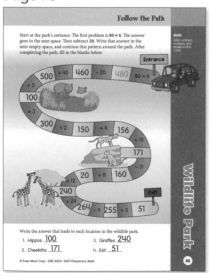

Page 94

Page 95

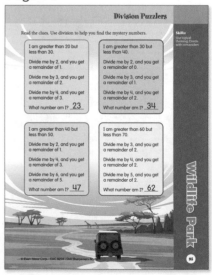

Page 96

Moms and Babies

Skill: Solve word problems

Solve the problems.

Flappy, a baby elephant, weighed 200 pounds at birth. Her mother was 30 times heavier!

How much did Flappy's mother weigh?

6,000 pounds

Nala, a newborn tiger cub, weighed 3 pounds. His mother was 240 pounds.

How many times heavier was the mother than her cub?

80 times heavier

A five-month-old hippo weighed 300 pounds. That was only $\frac{1}{10}$ the weight of her mother.

How much did the mother hippo weigh?

3,000 pounds

A one-year-old lion cub weighed 50 pounds. His mother weighed 6 times more.

How much did the lion cub's mother weigh?

300 pounds

Patch, a baby giraffe, weighed 150 pounds. His mother was 16 times heavier.

How much did Patch's mother weigh?

2,400 pounds

A mother zebra weighed 750 pounds. Her baby was only $\frac{1}{10}$ her weight.

How much did the baby zebra weigh?

75 pounds

Wildlife Park

96

Page 97

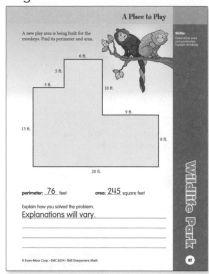

A Place to Play

Skills: Determine area and perimeter; Explain thinking

A new play area is being built for the monkeys. Find its perimeter and area.

perimeter: **76** feet   area: **245** square feet

Explain how you solved the problem.

Explanations will vary.

Wildlife Park

97

Page 98

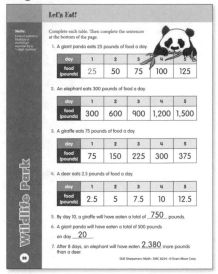

Let's Eat!

Skills: Extend patterns; Multiply a multidigit number by a 1-digit number

Complete each table. Then complete the sentences at the bottom of the page.

1. A giant panda eats 25 pounds of food a day.

day	1	2	3	4	5
food (pounds)	25	50	75	100	125

2. An elephant eats 300 pounds of food a day.

day	1	2	3	4	5
food (pounds)	300	600	900	1,200	1,500

3. A giraffe eats 75 pounds of food a day.

day	1	2	3	4	5
food (pounds)	75	150	225	300	375

4. A deer eats 2.5 pounds of food a day.

day	1	2	3	4	5
food (pounds)	2.5	5	7.5	10	12.5

5. By day 10, a giraffe will have eaten a total of **750** pounds.

6. A giant panda will have eaten a total of 500 pounds on day **20**.

7. After 8 days, an elephant will have eaten **2,380** more pounds than a deer.

Wildlife Park

98

Page 99

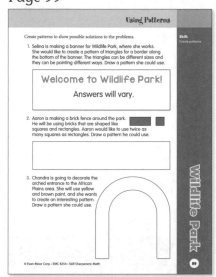

Using Patterns

Skill: Create patterns

Create patterns to show possible solutions to the problems.

1. Selina is making a banner for Wildlife Park, where she works. She would like to create a pattern of triangles for a border along the bottom of the banner. The triangles can be different sizes and they can be pointing different ways. Draw a pattern she could use.

Welcome to Wildlife Park!

Answers will vary.

2. Aaron is making a brick fence around the park. He will be using bricks that are shaped like squares and rectangles. Aaron would like to use twice as many squares as rectangles. Draw a pattern he could use.

3. Chandra is going to decorate the arched entrance to the African Plains area. She will use yellow and brown paint, and she wants to create an interesting pattern. Draw a pattern she could use.

Wildlife Park

99

Page 100

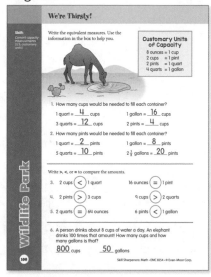

We're Thirsty!

Skill: Convert capacity measurements (U.S. customary units)

Write the equivalent measures. Use the information in the box to help you.

Customary Units of Capacity
8 ounces = 1 cup
2 cups = 1 pint
2 pints = 1 quart
4 quarts = 1 gallon

1. How many cups would be needed to fill each container?

1 quart = **4** cups   1 gallon = **16** cups

3 quarts = **12** cups   2 pints = **4** cups

2. How many pints would be needed to fill each container?

1 quart = **2** pints   1 gallon = **8** pints

5 quarts = **10** pints $2\frac{1}{2}$ gallons = **20** pints

Write >, <, or = to compare the amounts.

3. 2 cups **<** 1 quart   16 ounces **=** 1 pint

4. 2 pints **>** 3 cups   9 cups **>** 2 quarts

5. 2 quarts **=** 64 ounces   6 pints **<** 1 gallon

6. A person drinks about 8 cups of water a day. An elephant drinks 100 times that amount! How many cups and how many gallons is that?

800 cups   **50** gallons

Wildlife Park

100

Page 101

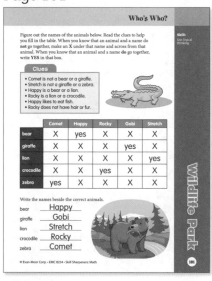

Who's Who?

Skill: Use logical thinking

Figure out the names of the animals below. Read the clues to help you fill in the table. When you know that an animal and a name do **not** go together, make an X under that name and across from that animal. When you know that an animal and a name **do** go together, write **YES** in that box.

Clues
• Comet is not a bear or a giraffe.
• Stretch is not a giraffe or a zebra.
• Happy is a bear or a lion.
• Rocky is a lion or a crocodile.
• Happy likes to eat fish.
• Rocky does not have hair or fur.

	Comet	Happy	Rocky	Gobi	Stretch
bear	X	yes	X	X	X
giraffe	X	X	X	yes	X
lion	X	X	X	X	yes
crocodile	X	X	yes	X	X
zebra	yes	X	X	X	X

Write the names beside the correct animals.

bear **Happy**
giraffe **Gobi**
lion **Stretch**
crocodile **Rocky**
zebra **Comet**

Wildlife Park

101

Page 102

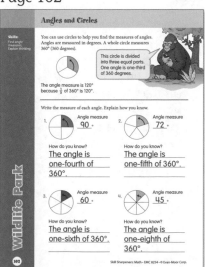

Angles and Circles

Skills: Find angle measure; Explain thinking

You can use circles to help you find the measures of angles. Angles are measured in degrees. A whole circle measures 360° (360 degrees).

This circle is divided into three equal parts. One angle is one-third of 360 degrees.

The angle measure is 120° because $\frac{1}{3}$ of 360° is 120°.

Write the measure of each angle. Explain how you know.

1. Angle measure **90**
How do you know?
The angle is one-fourth of 360°.

2. Angle measure **72**
How do you know?
The angle is one-fifth of 360°.

3. Angle measure **60**
How do you know?
The angle is one-sixth of 360°.

4. Angle measure **45**
How do you know?
The angle is one-eighth of 360°.

Wildlife Park

102

Page 103

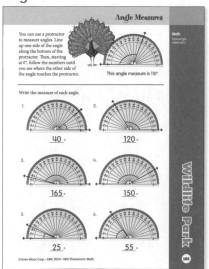

Angle Measures

Skill: Find angle measures

You can use a protractor to measure angles. Line up one side of the angle along the bottom of the protractor. Then, starting at 0°, follow the numbers until you see where the other side of the angle touches the protractor.

This angle measure is 110°.

Write the measure of each angle.

1. **40**°
2. **120**°
3. **165**°
4. **150**°
5. **25**°
6. **55**°

Wildlife Park

103

Page 104

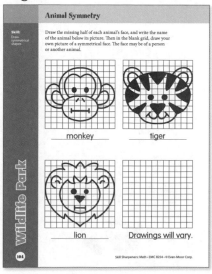

Animal Symmetry

Skill: Draw symmetrical shapes

Draw the missing half of each animal's face, and write the name of the animal below its picture. Then in the blank grid, draw your own picture of a symmetrical face. The face may be of a person or another animal.

monkey   tiger

lion   Drawings will vary.

Wildlife Park

104

Page 105

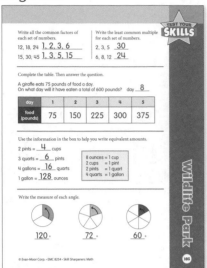

TEST YOUR SKILLS

Write all the common factors of each set of numbers.

12, 18, 24 **1, 2, 3, 6**

15, 30, 45 **1, 3, 5, 15**

Write the least common multiple for each set of numbers.

2, 3, 5 **30**

6, 8, 12 **24**

Complete the table. Then answer the question.

A giraffe eats 75 pounds of food a day.
On what day will it have eaten a total of 600 pounds? day **8**

day	1	2	3	4	5
food (pounds)	75	150	225	300	375

Use the information in the box to help you write equivalent amounts.

2 pints = **4** cups

3 quarts = **6** pints

4 gallons = **16** quarts

1 gallon = **128** ounces

8 ounces = 1 cup
2 cups = 1 pint
2 pints = 1 quart
4 quarts = 1 gallon

Write the measure of each angle.

120°   **72°**   **60°**

Wildlife Park

Page 106

A Bicycle Riddle

Why can't bicycles stand by themselves?

To solve the riddle, first write the sums for the problems below.
Then write the matching letters on the lines at the bottom of the page.

T 1,407 + 21,209 = **22,616**

E 9,519 + 45 = **9,564**

E 913 + 289 = **1,202**

R 45 + 132 + 5,084 = **5,261**

I 256 + 250 + 831 = **1,337**

O 290 + 491 + 502 = **1,283**

Y 805 + 75 + 9,490 = **10,370**

D 1,899 + 307 + 804 = **3,010**

T 6,503 + 7,303 = **13,806**

T 802 + 407 + 842 = **2,051**

E 735 + 285 + 482 = **1,502**

A 375 + 493 + 263 = **1,131**

R 907 + 32 + 284 = **1,223**

W 280 + 481 + 427 = **1,188**

H 285 + 429 + 492 = **1,206**

Because **T H E Y**
22,616 · 1,206 · 9,564 · 10,370

A R E   T W O
1,131 · 5,261 · 1,202 · 13,806 · 1,188 · 1,283

T I R E D
2,051 · 1,337 · 1,223 · 1,502 · 3,010

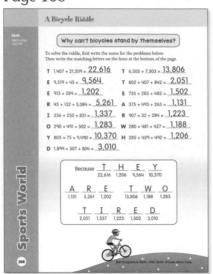

Sports World

Page 107

Ticket Maze

Jayden needs to get from the park entrance to the stadium. In order to walk along any path, he must give the gatekeeper the number of tickets that are noted on the path. Jayden has 98 tickets. He must use all of them to enter the stadium. Which paths can he follow to the stadium? Trace over the paths to show your answer.

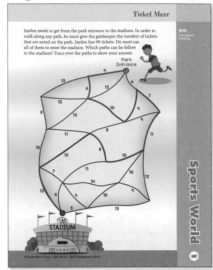

Sports World

Page 108

Knock 'Em Down!

Write the next three numbers in each pattern to knock down the pins in each bowling lane.

31,892 32,892 33,892 **34,892 35,892 36,892**

11,025 11,050 11,075 **11,100 11,125 11,150**

57,550 57,660 57,770 **57,880 57,990 58,100**

84,004 84,003 84,002 **84,001 84,000 83,999**

69,939 69,929 69,919 **69,909 69,899 69,889**

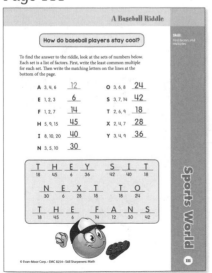

Sports World

Page 109

Sports Practice

Solve the problems.

Brianna goes to soccer practice every day. Each time, she practices for one hour. So far today, she has practiced for $\frac{1}{3}$ hour.
What fraction of an hour is left until her practice is over?
$\frac{2}{3}$ hour

How many minutes is that?
40 minutes

Yumi practices swimming at the local community pool. The pool is twice as long as it is wide.
The perimeter of the pool is 150 feet. What is the pool's length? What is its width?
length **50** feet
width **25** feet

Ian practices basketball with his friend. He usually shoots 8 baskets at every practice.
How many baskets would he shoot after 15 practices?
120 baskets

How many practices would it take for him to shoot 200 baskets?
25 practices

Raj practices tennis three times a week. Each time he practices for $1\frac{1}{2}$ hours.
How many hours does Raj practice tennis in one week?
$4\frac{1}{2}$ hours

Suppose Raj practiced for a total of 18 hours. How many practices was that?
12 practices

Sports World

Page 110

At the Track Meet

Some runners are ready to compete at the track meet. The Venn diagram shows the number of runners for two races.

100-meter race   relay race
18 | 6 | 14

1. How many runners will compete in **only** the 100-meter race? **18** runners

2. How many runners will compete in **only** the relay race? **14** runners

3. How many runners in all will compete in the 100-meter race? **24** runners

4. How many runners in all will compete in the relay race? **20** runners

5. How many runners will compete in at least one race? **38** runners

6. Suppose a runner who was planning to run in both races drops out because of illness. What might the Venn diagram look like then? Write your answer below.

100-meter race   relay race
18 | 5 | 14

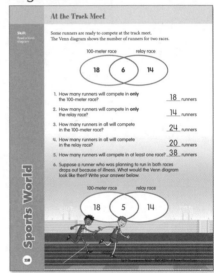

Sports World

Page 111

A Baseball Riddle

How do baseball players stay cool?

To find the answer to the riddle, look at the sets of numbers below. Each set is a list of factors. First, write the least common multiple for each set. Then write the matching letters on the lines at the bottom of the page.

A 3, 4, 6 **12**

E 1, 2, 3 **6**

F 1, 2, 7 **14**

H 5, 9, 15 **45**

I 8, 10, 20 **40**

N 3, 5, 10 **30**

O 3, 6, 8 **24**

S 3, 7, 14 **42**

T 2, 6, 9 **18**

X 2, 4, 7 **28**

Y 3, 4, 9 **36**

T H E Y   S I T
18 · 45 · 6 · 36 · · 42 · 40 · 18

N E X T   T O
30 · 6 · 28 · 18 · · 18 · 24

T H E   F A N S
18 · 45 · 6 · · 14 · 12 · 30 · 42

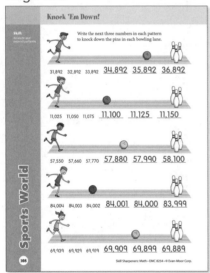

Sports World

Page 112

What's Your Estimate?

Give an estimate for each answer below. Do **not** compute the exact answer. Then use numbers or words to explain how you made your estimate.

What is a good estimate for 11 × 35?
350 estimate
Explain.
It's close to 10 × 35.

What is a good estimate for the sum of 299 and 503?
800 estimate
Explain.
It's close to 300 + 500.

What is a good estimate for 604 − 98?
500 estimate
Explain.
It's close to 600 − 100.

What is a good estimate for the product of 8,013 and 2?
16,000 estimate
Explain.
It's close to 8,000 × 2.

What is a good estimate for how many times 9 goes into 2,675?
300 estimate
Explain.
It's close to 2,700 ÷ 9.

What is a good estimate for 1,971 and 4,156?
6,000 estimate
Explain.
It's close to 2,000 + 4,000.

Sports World

Page 113

Mei's Sport

Solve the problems. Then write the answers in order from smallest to largest on the lines below. Write the corresponding letter for each answer in the boxes to find out what sport Mei plays.

E 0.04 + 0.05 = **0.09**

A 0.27 + 1.19 = **1.46**

P 3.2 − 2.3 = **0.9**

G 5.65 − 2.6 = **3.05**

M 7.15 − 7.1 = **0.05**

F 1.04 + 3.48 = **4.52**

O 9.1 − 5.5 = **3.6**

L 0.08 + 1.12 = **1.20**

S 3.59 − 0.7 = **2.89**

I 1.09 − 0.99 = **0.10**

L 2.18 + 2.07 = **4.25**

Y 0.45 + 1.63 = **2.08**

0.05	0.09	0.10
M	E	I

0.9	1.20	1.46	2.08	2.89
P	L	A	Y	S

3.05	3.6	4.25	4.52
G	O	L	F

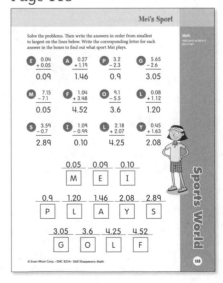

Sports World

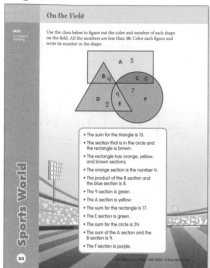

On the Field

Skill: Use logical thinking

Use the clues below to figure out the color and number of each shape on the field. All the numbers are less than 10. Color each figure and write its number in the shape.

A 5
B 4
C 8
D 2
E 9
7
F

- The sum for the triangle is 15.
- The section that is in the circle and the rectangle is brown.
- The rectangle has orange, yellow, and brown sections.
- The orange section is the number 4.
- The product of the B section and the blue section is 8.
- The 9 section is green.
- The A section is yellow.
- The sum for the rectangle is 17.
- The E section is green.
- The sum for the circle is 24.
- The sum of the A section and the B section is 9.
- The F section is purple.

Sports World

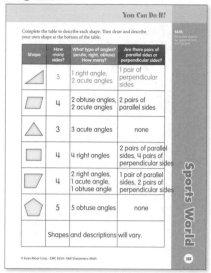

You Can Do It!

Complete the table to describe each shape. Then draw and describe your own shape at the bottom of the table.

Shape	How many sides?	What type of angles? (acute, right, obtuse) How many?	Are there pairs of parallel sides or perpendicular sides?
	3	1 right angle, 2 acute angles	1 pair of perpendicular sides
	4	2 obtuse angles, 2 acute angles	2 pairs of parallel sides
	3	3 acute angles	none
	4	4 right angles	2 pairs of parallel sides, 4 pairs of perpendicular sides
	4	2 right angles, 1 acute angle, 1 obtuse angle	1 pair of parallel sides, 2 pairs of perpendicular sides
	5	5 obtuse angles	none
	Shapes and descriptions will vary.		

Sports World

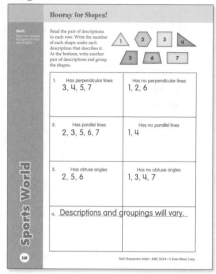

Hooray for Shapes!

Read the pair of descriptions in each row. Write the number of each shape under each description that describes it. At the bottom, write another pair of descriptions and group the shapes.

1 2 3 4 5 6 7

1. Has perpendicular lines 3, 4, 5, 7	Has no perpendicular lines 1, 2, 6
2. Has parallel lines 2, 3, 5, 6, 7	Has no parallel lines 1, 4
3. Has obtuse angles 2, 5, 6	Has no obtuse angles 1, 3, 4, 7
4. Descriptions and groupings will vary.	

Sports World

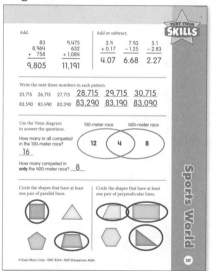

TEST YOUR SKILLS

Add.

```
    83        9,475
 8,964          632
+  758       +1,084
-----        ------
9,805        11,191
```

Add or subtract.

```
  3.9      7.93      5.1
+0.17     -1.25    -2.83
-----     -----    -----
 4.07      6.68     2.27
```

Write the next three numbers in each pattern.

25,715 26,715 27,715 **28,715 29,715 30,715**

83,590 83,490 83,390 **83,290 83,190 83,090**

Use the Venn diagram to answer the questions.

100-meter race   400-meter race
12   4   8

How many in all competed in the 100-meter race? **16**

How many competed in only the 400-meter race? **8**

Circle the shapes that have at least one pair of parallel lines.

Circle the shapes that have at least one pair of perpendicular lines.

Sports World

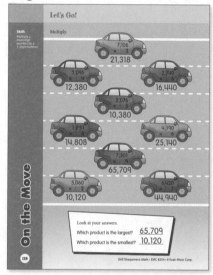

Let's Go!

Skill: Multiply a multidigit number by a 1-digit number.

Multiply.

7,106 × 3 = 21,318
3,095 × 4 = 12,380
2,746 × 6 = 16,440
2,076 × 5 = 10,380
1,851 × 8 = 14,808
4,190 × 6 = 25,140
7,301 × 9 = 65,709
5,060 × 2 = 10,120
6,420 × 7 = 44,940

Look at your answers.
Which product is the largest? **65,709**
Which product is the smallest? **10,120**

On the Move

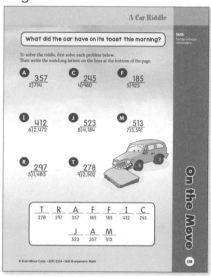

A Car Riddle

What did the car have on its toast this morning?

Skill: Divide without remainders.

To solve the riddle, first solve each problem below. Then write the matching letters on the lines at the bottom of the page.

A 357 2)714
C 245 4)980
F 185 5)925
I 412 6)2,472
J 523 8)4,184
M 513 7)3,591
R 297 5)1,485
T 278 9)2,502

T	R	A	F	F	I	C
278	297	357	185	185	412	245

J	A	M
523	357	513

On the Move

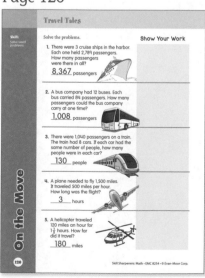

Travel Tales

Skill: Solve word problems.

Solve the problems.

Show Your Work

1. There were 3 cruise ships in the harbor. Each one held 2,789 passengers. How many passengers were there in all?
8,367 passengers

2. A bus company had 12 buses. Each bus carried 84 passengers. How many passengers could the bus company carry at one time?
1,008 passengers

3. There were 1,040 passengers on a train. The train had 8 cars. If each car had the same number of people, how many people were in each car?
130 people

4. A plane needed to fly 1,500 miles. It traveled 500 miles per hour. How long was the flight?
3 hours

5. A helicopter traveled 120 miles an hour for 1½ hours. How far did it travel?
180 miles

On the Move

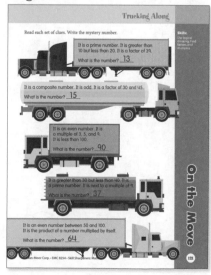

Trucking Along

Skill: Use logical thinking. Find factors and multiples.

Read each set of clues. Write the mystery number.

It is a prime number. It is greater than 10 but less than 20. It is a factor of 39.
What is the number? **13**

It is a composite number. It is odd. It is a factor of 30 and 45.
What is the number? **15**

It is an even number. It is a multiple of 3, 5, and 9. It is less than 100.
What is the number? **90**

It is greater than 30 and less than 40. It is a prime number. It is next to a multiple of 9.
What is the number? **37**

It is an even number between 50 and 100. It is the product of a number multiplied by itself.
What is the number? **64**

On the Move

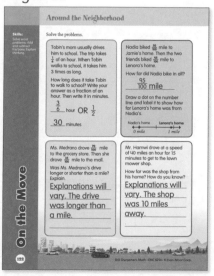

Around the Neighborhood

Skills: Solve word problems. Add and subtract fractions. Explain thinking.

Solve the problems.

Tobin's mom usually drives him to school. The trip takes ¼ of an hour. When Tobin walks to school, it takes him 3 times as long.

How long does it take Tobin to walk to school? Write your answer as a fraction of an hour. Then write it in minutes.
3/6 hour OR **½**
30 minutes

Nadia biked 45/100 mile to Jamie's home. Then the two friends biked 50/100 mile to Lenora's home.

How far did Nadia bike in all?
95/100 mile

Draw a dot on the number line and label it to show how far Lenora's home was from Nadia's.

Nadia's home ——— Lenora's home
0 mile   1 mile

Ms. Medrano drove 30/100 mile to the grocery store. Then she drove 80/100 mile to the mall.

Was Ms. Medrano's drive longer or shorter than a mile? Explain.
Explanations will vary. The drive was longer than a mile.

Mr. Hamwi drove at a speed of 40 miles an hour for 15 minutes to get to the lawn mower shop.

How far was the shop from his home? How do you know?
Explanations will vary. The shop was 10 miles away.

On the Move

Page 123

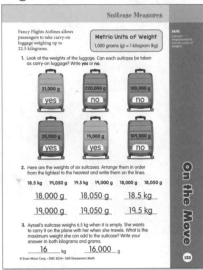

Suitcase Measures

Fancy Flights Airlines allows passengers to take carry-on luggage weighing up to 22.5 kilograms.

Skill: Convert measurements (metric units of weight)

Metric Units of Weight
1,000 grams (g) = 1 kilogram (kg)

1. Look at the weights of the luggage. Can each suitcase be taken as carry-on luggage? Write **yes** or **no.**

- 21,000 g — yes
- 220,000 g — no
- 100,000 g — no
- 20,000 g — yes
- 19,000 g — yes
- 109,000 g — no

2. Here are the weights of six suitcases. Arrange them in order from the lightest to the heaviest and write them on the lines.

18.5 kg   19,050 g   18.5 kg   19,000 g   18,000 g   18,050 g

18,000 g   18,050 g   18.5 kg
19,000 g   19,050 g   19.5 kg

3. Ayssel's suitcase weighs 6.5 kg when it is empty. She wants to carry it on the plane with her when she travels. What is the maximum weight she can add to the suitcase? Write your answer in both kilograms and grams.

16 kg   16,000 g

© Evan-Moor Corp. • EMC 8254 • Skill Sharpeners: Math

On the Move — 123

Page 124

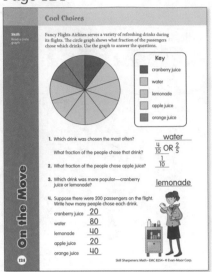

Cool Choices

Skill: Read a circle graph

Fancy Flights Airlines serves a variety of refreshing drinks during its flights. The circle graph shows what fraction of the passengers chose which drinks. Use the graph to answer the questions.

Key
- cranberry juice
- water
- lemonade
- apple juice
- orange juice

1. Which drink was chosen the most often? **water** — $\frac{4}{10}$ OR $\frac{2}{5}$

What fraction of the people chose that drink?

2. What fraction of the people chose apple juice? $\frac{1}{10}$

3. Which drink was more popular—cranberry juice or lemonade? **lemonade**

4. Suppose there were 200 passengers on the flight. Write how many people chose each drink.

cranberry juice — 20
water — 80
lemonade — 40
apple juice — 20
orange juice — 20

Skill Sharpeners: Math • EMC 8254 • © Evan-Moor Corp.

On the Move — 124

Page 125

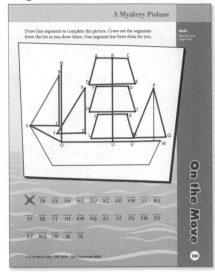

A Mystery Picture

Skill: Identify line segments

Draw line segments to complete the picture. Cross out the segments from the list as you draw them. One segment has been done for you.

X̶	TR	UV	FH	NO	OU	XZ	AD	VW	LJ	BU
ST	DE	CE	HI	KM	PQ	AC	YZ	FG	PM	SO
XY	MQ	LM	JK	GI						

© Evan-Moor Corp. • EMC 8254 • Skill Sharpeners: Math

On the Move — 125

Page 126

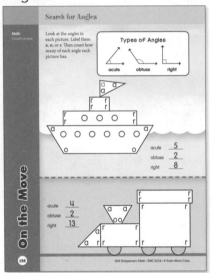

Search for Angles

Skill: Classify angles

Look at the angles in each picture. Label them **a, o,** or **r.** Then count how many of each angle each picture has.

Types of Angles
acute   obtuse   right

acute — 5
obtuse — 2
right — 8

acute — 4
obtuse — 2
right — 13

126 — **On the Move**

Skill Sharpeners: Math • EMC 8254 • © Evan-Moor Corp.

Page 127

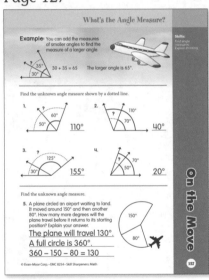

What's the Angle Measure?

Skills: Find angle measures; Explain thinking

Example You can add the measures of smaller angles to find the measure of a larger angle.

30 + 35 = 65   The larger angle is 65°.

Find the unknown angle measure shown by a dotted line.

1. 60° / 50° → 110°
2. 110° / 70° → 40°
3. 125° / 30° → 155°
4. 70° / 50° → 20°

Find the unknown angle measure.

5. A plane circled an airport waiting to land. It moved around 150° and then another 80°. How many more degrees will the plane travel before it returns to its starting position? Explain your answer.

The plane will travel 130°.
A full circle is 360°.
360 – 150 – 80 = 130

© Evan-Moor Corp. • EMC 8254 • Skill Sharpeners: Math

On the Move — 127

Page 128

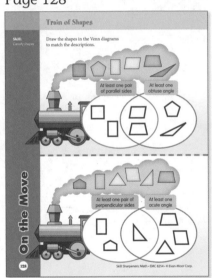

Train of Shapes

Skill: Classify shapes

Draw the shapes in the Venn diagrams to match the descriptions.

At least one pair of parallel sides   At least one obtuse angle

At least one pair of perpendicular sides   At least one acute angle

128 — **On the Move**

Skill Sharpeners: Math • EMC 8254 • © Evan-Moor Corp.

Page 129

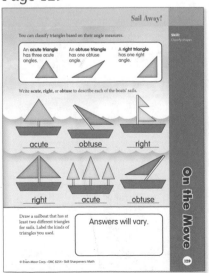

Sail Away!

Skill: Classify shapes

You can classify triangles based on their angle measures.

An **acute triangle** has three acute angles.

An **obtuse triangle** has one obtuse angle.

A **right triangle** has one right angle.

Write **acute, right,** or **obtuse** to describe each of the boats' sails.

- acute
- obtuse
- right
- right
- acute
- obtuse

Draw a sailboat that has at least two different triangles for sails. Label the kinds of triangles you used.

Answers will vary.

© Evan-Moor Corp. • EMC 8254 • Skill Sharpeners: Math

On the Move — 129

Page 130

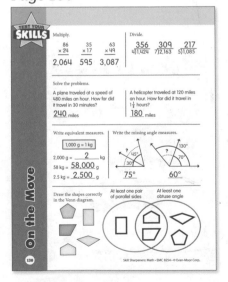

TEST YOUR SKILLS

Multiply.

$\begin{array}{r} 86 \\ \times 24 \\ \hline 2{,}064 \end{array}$ $\begin{array}{r} 35 \\ \times 17 \\ \hline 595 \end{array}$ $\begin{array}{r} 63 \\ \times 49 \\ \hline 3{,}087 \end{array}$

Divide.

$4\overline{)1{,}424} = 356$ $7\overline{)2{,}163} = 309$ $5\overline{)1{,}085} = 217$

Solve the problems.

A plane traveled at a speed of 480 miles an hour. How far did it travel in 30 minutes? **240** miles

A helicopter traveled at 120 miles an hour. How far did it travel in $1\frac{1}{2}$ hours? **180** miles

Write equivalent measures.

1,000 g = 1 kg

2,000 g = **2** kg
58 kg = **58,000** g
2.5 kg = **2,500** g

Write the missing angle measures.

45° / 30° → **75°**
130° / 70° → **60°**

Draw the shapes correctly in the Venn diagram.

At least one pair of parallel sides   At least one obtuse angle

130 — **On the Move**

Skill Sharpeners: Math • EMC 8254 • © Evan-Moor Corp.